TO IMRAN

DO NOT WAIT FOR

TO-MORROW

FOR IT IS TO-DAY.

HAPPY READING.

LOVE
HASHIM
xxx

INVOCATIONS AND SUPPLICATIONS

Kitāb al-adhkār wa'l-daᶜawāt

Book IX of the Revival of the Religious Sciences

Iḥyā' ᶜUlūm al-Dīn

AL-GHAZĀLĪ

INVOCATIONS & SUPPLICATIONS

Kitāb al-adhkār wa'l-daᶜawāt · BOOK IX of THE REVIVAL OF THE RELIGIOUS SCIENCES *Iḥyā' ᶜulūm al-dīn* · translated with an INTRODUCTION & Notes by K. NAKAMURA

THE ISLAMIC TEXTS SOCIETY
CAMBRIDGE 1990

The Islamic Texts Society
5 Green Street
Cambridge
CB2 3JU, U.K.

British Library Cataloguing in Publication Data
Ghazālī, Abū Ḥāmid Muḥammad ibn Muḥammad al-
The Book of Invocations and Supplications
Second revised edition
1. Islamic life—Prayer
I. Title II. Nakamura, Kojiro
III. Iḥyā' ʿUlūm al-Dīn
(Kitāb al-adhkār wa'l-daʿawāt)
English
297'.43

ISBN 0 946621 12 8 cased

ISBN 0 946621 14 4 paper

Printed in the United Kingdom.

Publication of this volume has been made possible
by the generous support of Dar al-Maal al-Islami,
Geneva.

EDITOR'S NOTE

In preparing this text for republication as part of the Islamic Texts Society's series of translations from the *Iḥyā'*, a number of modifications to the Tokyo edition of 1973 have been carried out. The *ḥadīth* material has been identified, with the able assistance of Muḥammad ʿAbd al-Laṭīf and Muḥsin al-Najjār of Cairo, and is now referenced in notes at the end of the book, which also include the more important variant readings. Professor Nakamura's biographies of the personalities cited in the text have been assembled in alphabetical order as a new Appendix. A short excursus which appeared as Appendices I and II in the Tokyo edition has been omitted, while the Bibliography has been restructured and somewhat abbreviated. Finally, the translation itself has been amended in a few places, to bring it into greater conformity with the style adopted for the other works of this Series.

Professor Nakamura has lately been appointed Head of the Islamic Studies Department at Tokyo University, and the concomitant workload has made it impossible for him to carry out the above restructuring himself. It has, however, benefited from his full support and encouragement.

T J Winter
Cambridge
January 1990

PREFACE

Here presented to the English-speaking public is a translation of the ninth of the forty 'books' of Ghazālī's great work, *Iḥyā' ᶜulūm al-dīn*. It is entitled *Kitāb al-Adhkār wa'l-daᶜawāt* (*The Book of Invocations and Supplications*). This translation was originally part of my doctoral dissertation on this great Muslim thinker, submitted to Harvard University in 1970. It is a pleasant duty to express my thanks to, among others, Professors Annemarie Schimmel, Wilfred Cantwell Smith, George Makdisi, Ilse Lichtenstadter of Harvard University, Dr. Herbert Mason of Boston University, and the Reverend Patrick Ryan, SJ, who all generously gave me various forms of help and encouragement while I was working on the dissertation; particularly Professor Schimmel, who guided me all through my thesis work.

Unfortunately we have so far no critically edited standard text of the *Iḥyā'*. I have used for the present translation four texts available to me: (1) the text published by ᶜĪsā al-Bābī al-Ḥalabī (abbreviated IH), Cairo, n.d., with an introduction (dated 1379 AH/1957 AD) by Badawī Ṭabbāna, 4 vols.; (2) the text published by the Lajna Nashr al-Thaqāfa al-Islāmīya (TH), Cairo, 1356–57 AH, 5 vols.; (3) the text shown by Zabīdī in his commentary on the *Iḥyā'*, namely, *Itḥāf al-sādat al-muttaqīn bi-sharḥ asrār Iḥyā' ᶜulūm al-dīn*, published by al-Maṭbaᶜa al-Maymanīya (Z), Cairo, 1311 AH, 10 vols.; and (4) the text on the margin of the *Itḥāf* (ZM), which the publisher of the *Itḥāf* added since the text Z is not complete. This text ZM is relatively the most reliable of all, but none of the four is free from defects one way or another. The variants in the texts are shown in the footnotes, except the obvious typographical mistakes. As for the pagination in reference, quotation, and translation, I have followed that of the text IH.

I have consulted the English translations of the Qur'ān (abbreviated Q) by A.J. Arberry, R. Bell, M.M. Pickthall, and J.M. Rodwell, but none of them is used exclusively in reference and quotation. Verses are numbered according to the Cairo edition.

The square brackets in the translation are inserted by the translator to clarify the meaning for the reader. The round brackets are the insertions in the other text(s) as indicated in the footnotes.

Kojiro Nakamura
Tokyo
June 1972

CONTENTS

THE BOOK OF INVOCATIONS AND SUPPLICATIONS

ABBREVIATIONS

EI	:	*The Encyclopedia of Islam* (First edition)
EI^2	:	*The Encyclopedia of Islam* (Second edition)
GAL	:	Brockelmann, *Geschichte des arabischen Litteratur*
GALS	:	Brockelmann, *Geschichte* . . . (Supplement)
GAS	:	Sezgin, *Geschichte des arabischen Schrifttums*
Ḥākim	:	al-Ḥākim al-Nīsābūrī, *al-Mustadrak* . . .
Hujwīrī	:	Nicholson (tr.), *Kashf al-maḥjūb*
IQ	:	*The Islamic Quarterly*
Iṣāba	:	Ibn Ḥajar, *al-Iṣāba* . . .
Jalālayn	:	Suyūṭī and Maḥallī, *Tafsīr* . . .
JAOS	:	*Journal of the American Oriental Society*
Kāshif	:	al-Dhahabī, *al-Kāshif* . . .
MIDEO	:	*Mélanges de l'Institut Dominicain d'Études Orientales du Caire*
MW	:	*The Muslim World*
Q.	:	*al-Qur'ān al-Karīm*
Qūt	:	al-Makkī, *Qūt al-qulūb*
RA	:	*Revue Africaine*
RT	:	*Revue Thomiste*
SCR	:	*Studies in Comparative Religion*
SEI	:	*The Shorter Encyclopedia of Islam*
Tahdhīb al-Tahdhīb	:	Ibn Ḥajar, *Tahdhīb al-Tahdhīb*

Tārīkh Baghdād	:	al-Khaṭīb al-Baghdādī, *Tārīkh Baghdād*
WI	:	*Die Welt des Islams*
WZKM	:	*Wiener Zeitschrift für die Kunde des Morgenlandes*
ZDMG	:	*Zeitschrift der Deutschen Morgenländischen Gesellschaft*

INTRODUCTION

THE LIFE OF GHAZĀLĪ[1]

GHAZĀLĪ (or Ḥujjat al-Islām Abū Ḥāmid Muḥammad ibn Muḥammad ibn Muḥammad ibn Aḥmad al-Ṭūsī al-Ghazālī), one of the greatest and most original thinkers in the history of Islam, was born in 450 AH (1058 AD) and brought up in the north-eastern part of Persia. His father, and possibly his mother also, died early leaving him and his younger brother, Aḥmad, in their childhood. From an early age, according to his own account in *al-Munqidh min al-ḍalāl* (*'The Deliverer from Delusion'*), it was his habit and custom 'to thirst after a comprehension of things as they really are'.[2] He had already been intellectually too critically-minded and too self-confident to accept naïvely the traditional teachings as they were by the time he reached adolescence. Unable to be content with the given answers, he turned to verify the traditional beliefs and truths by himself, and thus became seriously engaged in studying every branch of the religious sciences (Qur'ānic studies, theology, philosophy, Islamic jurisprudence, and others) in search of Truth.

To a certain extent he was indeed successful in his quest; he mastered all these sciences, and was socially rewarded for his brilliant talents and endeavours. In 478, on the death of Imām al-Ḥaramayn, a great theologian and jurist of his age, under whom Ghazālī had been studying with other eminent students, he moved from Nīsābūr to the Camp of Niẓām al-Mulk, vizier of the Seljuqid Sultan. This vizier, surrounded by scholars and poets as their patron, was making efforts to restore Sunnī Islam with the support of Muslim intellectuals against the Shīʿism which was rampant at that time. Ghazālī was duly received, and in 484 was appointed professor at the Niẓāmīya

College (*Madrasa*) of Baghdad, the highest position and the most coveted honour for the Muslim scholars of those days. Thus he put himself in the midst of the political and ideological battles and intrigues which were taking place in the imperial city of Baghdad. He set out as a champion of Sunnī Islam to refute in a series of his works Ismāᶜīlī Shīᶜism and philosophy (*falsafa*) which threatened to undermine the Sunnī establishment both politically and ideologically.

Along with, or rather as a result of, all this success and his thoroughgoing intellectual and logical pursuit, however, he came to realize that he was still devoid of the true faith (*yaqīn*),[3] or experimental understanding (*dhawq*) of the truth which he had so far been pursuing, demonstrating, and teaching; namely, the unity of God (*tawḥīd*) expressed in the Muslim confession: 'There is no god but God; Muḥammad is the Emissary of God' and the life in the Hereafter. To put it epistemologically, Ghazālī fell into deep scepticism and found himself desperately struggling to find the solid basis for knowledge of religious truth.[4] Ethically he came to be aware of, and to admit with daring frankness, the gap between his actual way of life and the imperative of God as he understood it.[5] And he also realized that this gap could not be bridged by intellectual effort, and that true faith was a divine gift freely bestowed by God upon the Sufi in the ecstatic experience of *fanā'* ('passing away').[6] In this mystical experience, the Sufi intuitively knows his own nothingness and absolute dependence upon God, and the overwhelming reality and universal sovereignty of God (*tawḥīd*). All man can, and should, do is to prepare himself to wait for this grace by detaching himself and emptying his thought and will of all concerns but God.

After these acute inner crises and the agonizing process of decision, Ghazālī finally renounced his position, honour, family, wealth, and all that would obstruct his devotion to God, and left Baghdad in the (eleventh) month of Dhu'l-Qaᶜda, 488, ostensibly to make the pilgrimage to Mecca. He went to Syria, and stayed there 'for nearly two years',[7] wandering as a hermit in Damascus, Jerusalem, Hebron, and possibly Alexandria. In the meantime he joined the pilgrimage of 489. Then, after another short stay in Damascus, he went back to Baghdad before the (sixth) month of Jumādā II, 490, and then returned to his native town. He continued the Sufi practices there with a small number of his disciples,[8] while composing many works, for about ten years until his death in 505 AH (1111 AD), except for a short period of teaching at the Niẓāmīya College of Nīsābūr, towards the end of his life.

THE *IḤYĀ' ᶜULŪM AL-DĪN*

The *Iḥyā' ᶜUlūm al-Dīn* ('Revivification of the Religious Sciences'), his *magnum opus* and the Muslim counterpart of the *Summa Theologiae*, was composed during this period of retreat, possibly during the years 489–495, according to M. Bouyges;[9] that is to say, he started working on this great work in less than a year after leaving Baghdad, and it took him almost six years, while he was assiduous in the Sufi practices. It is, therefore, quite natural to suppose that the *Iḥyā'* reflects G͟hazālī's inner spiritual development and his new thought on the various branches of Islamic studies after his conversion. And in fact it does in my judgement. As such the *Iḥyā'* is vital to an understanding of the whole system of G͟hazālī's thought, as well as having great importance in the later history of Islamic thought.[10]

As for the contents, the work is divided into four quarters (*rubᶜ*), and each quarter into ten books (*kitāb*), as shown below:

QUARTER I: *The Acts of Worship* (ᶜIbādāt)

Book 1. On Knowledge
Book 2. On the Articles of Faith

QUARTER II: *The Norms of Daily Life* (ᶜĀdāt)

QUARTER III: *The Ways to Perdition* (Muhlikāt)

QUARTER IV: *The Ways to Salvation* (Munjīyāt)

Book 1. On Repentance
Book 2. On Patience and Gratitude
Book 3. On Fear and Hope
Book 4. On Poverty and Asceticism
Book 5. On Divine Unity and Dependence
Book 6. On Love, Longing, Intimacy and Contentment
Book 7. On Intention, Single-Heartedness and Sincerity
Book 8. On Self-Examination and Self-Account
Book 9. On Meditation
Book 10. On Remembrance of Death and the Afterlife

In the first quarter, entitled 'The Acts of Worship', Ghazālī first clarifies the meanings and functions of knowledge, and the orthodox dogma in outline, and then proceeds to expound the external forms and merits of the acts of worship, such as ablution (*ṭahāra*), ritual prayer (*ṣalāt*), fasting (*ṣawm*), pilgrimage (*ḥajj*), and so forth, while emphasizing their inner meanings and mysteries as he understands them. In the second, entitled 'The Norms of Daily Life', Ghazālī deals with the norms and ethics, again after the pattern of the Prophet, in the rest of the Muslim's daily activities, which are needed for his mundane existence and his devotion to God. In the third, entitled 'The Ways to Perdition', Ghazālī investigates the essential and cosmological nature of man and his ordinary states, and clarifies the evil traits of man which are obstructive to man's approach to God and his salvation in the Hereafter, together with the methods to remedy and correct them. In the fourth, entitled 'The Ways to Salvation', Ghazālī describes the various states and stages of man's spiritual development in his purgative way.

After all, the *Iḥyā'* is, in my view, a compendium of all Muslim religious sciences—theology (*kalām*), jurisprudence (*fiqh*), Qur'ān exegesis (*tafsīr*), the science of Tradition (*ᶜilm al-ḥadīth*), Sufism (*taṣawwuf*), etc.—interpreted and arranged from a single point of view: how to make preparations for 'seeing God' (*ru'yat Allāh*) or 'meeting with God' (*liqā' Allāh*) in the Hereafter. In other words, the *Iḥyā'* is an attempt to evaluate all the religious sciences according to the newly oriented Muslim way of life.

'A man dies in the same state as he has lived, and is resurrected in the same state as he has died.'[11] His heart (*qalb*)[12] leaves the human body on death. If it is free from worldly concerns in love of God in that moment, it immediately advances toward God. Otherwise, it cannot turn towards Him, being drawn back to the world by the love of it. What man should do, therefore, in this world is to make exertions to strengthen his love (*maḥabba*) of God and liberate himself from worldly bonds by using his bodily members[13] in imitation of the Prophetic pattern of Muḥammad, since he is the ideal model in this great enterprise. Once the heart is severed from the body, there is no remedy to remove its love of the world and to correct its worldly traits.

Dhikr (invocation) and *duᶜā'* (supplication) are two of the major methods in this purgative way. 'The Book of Invocations and Supplications' here translated is devoted to the theory and practical examples of them. Since these two concepts, apart from being the subject of the following translation, are important all through the rest of the *Iḥyā'*, we must now turn to an exposition of their whole structure.

DHIKR AND *DUᶜĀ'*

Dhikr

The word *dhikr* (from the verb *dhakara*) literally means 'to remember, recall' and 'to mention, utter'; that is, both man's mental activity and vocal communication. It is no wonder that in the Qur'ān these human actions are in most cases associated with God, the Creator. Man is commanded over and over again 'to remember' God, His works, and His favours.[14] *Dhikr* as vocal communication is often mentioned in connection with the worship of God in the sense of 'mentioning God's name', 'praising, glorifying Him by invoking His name'.[15] As such, it tends to be associated with particular places or occasions such as the mosque[16] and the ritual prayer (*ṣalāt*),[17] and even to be identified with the ritual prayer itself.[18] At the same time, the way of 'invoking God's name' became gradually specified and formalized, though there is no explicit statement in the Qur'ān about the formulas recited on specific occasions. Despite this process of reification or institutionalization, however, *dhikr* has never lost the aspect of a free, 'extra-canonical', devotional act in the Qur'ān.[19] It is in this last usage, together with the Qur'ānic exhortation of constant remembrance of God,[20] that it inspired the pious Muslims of the early generations.

Because of its great meritoriousness in expiating sins, *dhikr* as praise of God by invoking or calling upon His name was practised assiduously, together with repentance (*tawba*) and other ascetic exercises, by those early Muslims who were preoccupied with the idea of the approaching Last Judgement, in order to escape from the eternal doom of hellfire.[21] On the other hand, among the Sufis, who were the spiritual heirs of those early ascetics, the same *dhikr* continued to be observed not merely for such meritoriousness so much as for its promoting the concentration of the mind, in their effort toward the final goal of mystical experience (*fanā'*). Ghazālī is one of those who gave theoretical expression to this exercise of the *dhikr*. Later it underwent further development among the Sufi orders (*ṭuruq*, singular *ṭarīqa*), absorbing external influences, and came to be practised in groups as well as in solitude, with the accompaniment of various techniques: breathing, bodily movements, music, and others. Each order has come to be associated with a particular manner of *dhikr*, and thus *dhikr* has become the main distinctive practice of each Sufi order.[22]

The usages of the term *dhikr* in Ghazālī's thought are widely ranged from the general and Qur'ānic to the specifically Sufi meaning. We may group them into five categories. First of all, as man's mental or spiritual activity, *dhikr* is an endeavour to keep the mind in constant remembrance of God, or a laborious effort to turn one's concerns, preoccupied with worldly things, toward God by remembering Him constantly.[23] As long as man is occupied with the remembrance (*dhikr*) of God, he is free from worldly concerns, and thus there is little chance for Satanic insinuation and temptation (*waswās*). Indeed, the remembrance of God is the safest refuge from Satan.[24] Yet it is very hard to keep on remembering God all through daily life, especially for the beginner who is still preoccupied with this world. He easily slips back into heedlessness (*ghafla*) of God, and thus Satanic insinuation creeps in.[25]

Secondly, *dhikr* means a kind of 'spiritual exercise', or meditation on one's own death, the torment in the tomb, the eschatological events like the Last Judgement, God's punishment in Hell (in addition to those on earth), or His gracious gifts, eternal joy in Paradise, and the like.[26] This type of *dhikr* may seem to be similar to the previous one. However, the two are methodologically different from each other: the latter leads to the higher state of *dhikr*,[27] whereas the former produces a certain mood or sentiment in the heart: fear (*khawf*), gratitude (*shukr*), or hope (*rajā'*), and this mood in turn will become a spur for more earnest engagement in the remembrance (*dhikr*) of God and in other exercises as well. Ghazālī particularly urges the novice to be mindful of his own death, which may come at any moment, and of his perilous position before God, and what will occur to him thereafter. Then, says Ghazālī, his delight in, and attachment to, the transient world will disappear.[28] In this second type of *dhikr*, as remembrance or meditation, its object is for the most part something other than God Himself.

The practice of meditation will become more effective when it is repeated regularly. To be sure, this idea of repetition is also included in the connotations of *dhikr* (or *tadhakkur*), for it purports not only to remember a certain idea but also to establish it in one's heart as a real virtue by repeating the remembrance of it. A better understanding of the semantics of *dhikr* may be obtained by contrasting it with *fikr* (discursive meditation), another meditative exercise, which means the production of a new idea or knowledge by combining two known different ones.[29] Whereas *fikr* is heuristic, *dhikr* is self-preserving. If these two meditative exercises are employed together with regard to God, the novice is able not only to multiply his knowledge (*ᶜilm*) of Him, but to strengthen and establish it in his heart.[30] If the exercises are conducted with reference to the mercy of God, man's love of God will be increased; if they are done with reference to His majesty, man's fear of Him will be strengthened.

Thus, if a man makes supplication (*duᶜā'*), and practices Qur'ān-recitation (*qirā'a*) and even the vocal *dhikr* (see below) on a regular daily basis, with his thought fixed on the ideas expressed therein, then these ideas are gradually established in him, and all these practices serve as an effective method auxiliary to those two types of mental *dhikr* we have mentioned above. And this is one of the fundamental principles underlying Ghazālī's daily exercises, which consist of supplication, invocation, Qur'ān-recitation, and meditation (*al-waẓā'if al-arbaᶜa*).

Thirdly, *dhikr* means the repeated invocation of God's name or utterance of a sacred formula. In the Prophetic traditions the practice is commended because of its meritoriousness, particularly its 'sacramental' nature—so to speak—in expiating one's sins. For example:

> [The Emissary of God] said, 'If one says, "Glory be to God, and praise be to Him!" (*Subḥāna 'Llāh wa-bi-ḥamdihi*)[31] a hundred times a day, his sins shall fall from him, even though they are like the foam of the sea'.[32]

> It is related: 'When a man says, "There is no god but God" (*Lā ilāha illa 'Llāh*), the word comes on the leaf [of his book],[33] and passes by [the records of his] sin, erasing them, until it finds a good deed similar to itself, and then finally nestles down beside it'.[34]

G͟hazālī, however, does not confine himself to the merit of this *d͟hikr* as it is expounded in the Traditions, and tries to investigate and surmise the reason. His attitude toward it is interpretative. He rather regards the reported merit of *d͟hikr* as symbolic of the special inner state which is induced in the heart of the Sufi by its repeated utterance.[35]

It is essential, according to G͟hazālī, to pronounce the formula with presence of mind, without any discrepancy between the tongue and the inner state of the utterer, as a Tradition says, 'He who professes single-heartedly (*muk͟hliṣ^{an}*), "There is no god but God" will enter Paradise'.[36] The pronouncement of the formula must be done 'single-heartedly' or 'sincerely' (*ṣidq^{an}*), without there being any other object or purpose whatsoever in the heart (see below, 30n). And, moreover, this presence of the mind in *d͟hikr* must be constant, without interruption.[37] Otherwise there would be no use of *d͟hikr*. When the Sufi novice performs *d͟hikr*, his inner aspect must be exactly like that of one who is fighting for the single cause of God (*jihād*), without any other object in mind but the Blissful Vision of Him (*ru'yat Allāh*) in the Hereafter. This is the very state which is expressed by the formula: 'There is no god but God' (*tahlīl*).[38]

We may conclude from the above discussion that mental *d͟hikr* is more essential and cardinal than vocal *d͟hikr*, which—although important—is rather an auxiliary method or 'support' for mental *dhikr*. This idea of the primacy of the meditative aspect is also implied when the practice of *dhikr* is methodically and systematically organized in combination with other similar services—discursive meditation, Qur'ān-recitation, and supplication. By observing all these services in turn, the Sufi keeps his mind in constant remembrance of God, while averting the boredom (*malal*) which comes from the repetition of the same act.[39] Thus Ghazālī repeatedly stresses presence of mind during these practices, as well as *dhikr*.[40] *Dhikr* becomes useless when it is nothing but a movement of the tongue, with no mind in it.

Indeed, it is burdensome and requires constant effort to turn the mind to the practice of *dhikr* and keep on doing it. This is particularly so in the first stage of the Sufi novitiate when his mind is not yet bent on the practice completely. Nevertheless, as the formula is uttered repeatedly over a long period of time, with the mind on the remembrance of God, the practice of *dhikr* becomes in the end something familiar (*uns*) and palatable to his nature; the initial hardship in it gradually disappears, and joy, sweetness, or love (*ḥubb*) in it result instead. A certain food, for instance, no matter how repugnant and distasteful to one's nature at first, generally turns sweet and pleasant in the end, when one tries to eat it with every effort and continues the practice. In like manner, no matter how unpleasant and impracticable a certain act may seem at first, repeated practice will eventually render it pleasant and joyful, and finally turn it into second nature. The same is true with the practice of *dhikr*. It becomes in the end such a blissful thing that the Sufi cannot endure without it.[41]

When familiarity (*uns*) with *dhikr* of God and love (*ḥubb*) of it have taken firm root deep in the heart, man's thought and concern are cut off from all but God. This implies that he has attained the state of single-heartedness (*ikhlāṣ*).[42] The orientation of his whole personality is now totally reversed. This is the state which we imply by the fourth usage of *dhikr*.

It is the inner state reached as a result of constant practice of *dhikr*, both mental and vocal, and other ascetic practices as well. It is the higher spiritual state in which a man is solely bent on God and his mind is completely submerged in the thought of Him. This is what Ghazālī means when he says that 'the real essence of *dhikr* is established in the heart only after the heart is consolidated in the fear of God (*taqwā*) and purified from the blameworthy qualities'.[43] Now no matter what the Sufi may do, his mind and thought always turn to God. No effort is needed for the remembrance (*dhikr*) of God. He is freed from all wordly concerns.

The fifth usage of *dhikr* is the most intensified method of repeating incessantly the name of God (*Allāh*) or a simple phrase such as 'Glory be to God!' (*Subḥāna 'Llāh*), without being disturbed by any other thought whatsoever. While practising this *dhikr*, the Sufi eventually

> . . . comes to a state in which his effort to move his tongue drops off and it looks as if the word were flowing on his tongue all by itself. Then, let him adhere to this until any trace of motion is removed from his tongue and he finds his mind persevering in *dhikr*. Then, let him still adhere to this until the image of the word, its letters and shape are effaced from his mind and there remains the idea of the word alone in the mind, clinging to it, as if it were glued to the mind, without separating from it.[44]

In this process, we see the mind of the Sufi gradually concentrated and recollected upon the word of *dhikr* and what is expressed by it. Characteristic of this *dhikr* is that all such practices as Qur'ān-recitation, reading of the Prophetic Traditions, or supplication, which may distract the mind, are shunned; and that only a short simple phrase is used for *dhikr*. The word used is such that when it is uttered uninterruptedly the repetition soon becomes mechanical. And this mechanical and monotonous repetition holds the mind from engaging in logical and imaginative wanderings and thus from drifting away from the word of *dhikr*.

The Sufi can advance up to this point by his own will and effort (*ikhtiyār*).[45] But no-one is able to step further and attract the mercy of God. He has only to wait, bare and surrendered to God's initiative and His will, with his mind completely empty, until the light of the Truth illumines his inner heart. About this final state (*fanā'*), Ghazālī writes as follows:

> He is like one dumbfounded (*madhūsh*), absorbed in the sea of the direct witnessing (*ᶜayn al-shuhūd*), whose inner state resembles that of the ladies who cut their hands, witnessing the beauty of Joseph, when they were dumbfounded and their perceptions were gone.[46] The Sufis express this state by saying that 'he has passed away from himself' (*faniya ᶜan nafsihi*). Whenever a man has passed away from himself, he has passed away from all besides himself. Then it is as if he passed away from everything except the Witnessed One, and passed away from the act of witnessing. For the heart, whenever it turns aside to view the act of witnessing and itself as a witness, becomes heedless of the Witnessed One. And for he who is infatuated with a thing which he sees, there is no turning aside, in his state of absorption, toward his witnessing, nor toward his own self through which his vision comes, nor toward his heart in which his joy lies . . .[47]

This is the ecstatic state in which the object, or 'the Witnessed One', has so completely permeated and absorbed the mind of the subject that he is not conscious of himself, but only of the object. To be more precise, the subject does not have *his* consciousness of the object, since he is not conscious of himself. Nor is there consciousness of *his* witnessing of the object. Only the Witnessed One occupies his mind. In this state, therefore, there is no differentiation or disparity between the witness, the witnessed one, and the act of witnessing. This is the time when 'the true nature of the Truth' (*ḥaqīqat al-Ḥaqq*) manifests itself,[48] 'the True One' (*al-Wāḥid al-Ḥaqq*) is seen,[49] and 'the secret of the Divine Kingdom' (*sirr al-malakūt*) is revealed.[50] This is the goal of the Sufi way in this world.[51] There is no more need of *dhikr* than there is of the guide once the destination is reached. For *dhikr* presupposes the subject of *dhikr* (*dhākir*) and its object (*madhkūr*). When this disparity disappears, there is no *dhikr* any more.[52] In this mystical experience, the Sufi is given instantaneously a direct understanding, with unshaken conviction (*yaqīn*), of the truth about the overwhelming reality of God as well as man's utter dependence upon Him, and about the life in the Hereafter.[53]

However, this state does not last long. On coming back to his ordinary state of consciousness, the Sufi finds himself grasped by ardent desire (*shawq*) to meet his Beloved again and to have another taste of such a blissful experience. As he thus continues and repeats all these practices and experiences, his love of God becomes strengthened and established.

Duᶜā'

The term *duᶜā'* has also undergone some development, especially among the Sufis. Its main usage in the Qur'ān, however, is limited to 'supplication', '(humble) request'.[54] This is also its present usage in Muslim life, whether its object be mundane or spiritual. It is often used as a synonym for *su'āl* (asking).[55] Among the Sufis, however, *duᶜā'* is, besides earnest request for the spiritual grace of God, more or less the praise of God, or confidential talk (*munājāt*) between man and Him.[56]

One of the characteristics of the Qur'ānic usage of *duᶜā'* is that it is often regarded as identical with the worship of God (*ᶜibāda*),[57] as is *dhikr*. This is probably because *duᶜā'* is a major form of expression of man's relation to God outside (and within) the prescribed ritual prayer. Every kind of *duᶜā'* is made to God, as He has said, '*Supplicate to Me, and I will answer you*'[58] and '*Verily I am near. I respond to the* duʿā' *of the supplicant when he offers it to Me*'[59]—supplications for health, wealth, forgiveness of sins, salvation in the Hereafter, happiness and well-being in this life, and so forth.

In later periods, some of these supplications were grouped and given special names—'supplication for forgiveness' (*istighfār*),[60] 'refuge-taking' (*istiʿādha* or *taʿawwudh*),[61] and 'invocation for blessing upon the Prophet' (*taṣliya*).[62] There are some other specific forms of *duʿā'* which are combined with ritual prayer, such as 'supplication for rain' (*istisqā'*),[63] 'supplication for choice' (*ṣalāt al-istikhāra*),[64] 'supplication for a need' (*ṣalāt al-ḥāja*),[65] and others. For each of these occasions many prayers (*adʿiya ma'thūra*) are collected from among the Prophetic Traditions as well as from prayers of the ancient pious men and saints whose supplications were heard by God. These are handed down in many devotional works.[66]

However, Sufis, and mystics in general, are by definition people who have renounced the world and forsaken self-seeking wishes, or at least try to do so.[67] Therefore, it is mere folly for them to supplicate for earthly things, since they are worthless, transient, and nothing in their eyes.[68]

Thus, *duʿā'*, or supplication, itself seems to contradict the mystical ideal of absolute unification with the will of God—*tawakkul* (complete trust) and *riḍā* (contentment).

In fact, some hold that 'silence and forbearance under the fulfilment of the eternal Decree are more perfect, and contentment with the will of the Truth which has preceded is better'.[69] Ibn al-Mubārak, a Persian ascetic,[70] said, 'It is for about fifty years that I have not prayed nor wished that any one should pray for me'.[71] And also Rābiʿa, a famous woman saint, refused to supplicate to God to relieve her illness, because, in her judgement, it would be contrary to His will.[72]

On the other hand, the Prophet said, '*Duʿā'* is the marrow of worship'.[73] It is the essential form of man's relationship to God, for '*duʿā'* shows the state of servanthood (*ʿubūdīya*)'.[74] Thus,

Abū Ḥāzim al-Aᶜraj said, 'To be deprived of *duᶜā'* would be more painful for me than to be deprived of the answer',[75] and many leading Sufis also urged the devotee to make supplication trustfully.[76] All this shows not only the difficulty of addressing God and making *duᶜā'* to Him in the right manner,[77] but also the difference in the meaning and usage of *duᶜā'* according to author and context.[78]

Ghazālī takes it for granted that *duᶜā'* is essential to man's relationship with God. As long as man remains human, he cannot dispense with *duᶜā'* to Him. It is so vital in his human life that it is utterly inconceivable to reject *duᶜā'* because of the apparent contradiction or discrepancy between *duᶜā'* and the eternal Decree of God. In fact, *duᶜā'* itself is, to Ghazālī's mind, a part of the Decree of God.[79] There is no contradiction between them.

The removal of an affliction and procuring of divine mercy by making *duᶜā'* do not signify the revocation of the eternal Decree, for this 'revocation' of the affliction is also predetermined. *Duᶜā'*, therefore, is what Ghazālī calls a 'cause' (*sabab*), or an occasion, through which the eternal divine will is fulfilled. It is something like drinking water to quench thirst. Just as it is ridiculous for a man to expect that God will remove the thirst without his drinking water, so it is ridiculous to expect that God will remove his affliction without his making *duᶜā'*. Just as the shield deflects the arrow and the two work against each other, so *duᶜā'* and an affliction work against each other.[80] On the other hand, *duᶜā'* is one 'cause' for the fulfilment of the divine will, but not *the* 'cause'. *Duᶜā'* does not dispense with all other efforts on man's part, as does drinking water in order to quench thirst. It is not impossible that God could quench his thirst without his effort to drink water. But this is not God's Custom. Thus, it is absurd to expect divine response to his *duᶜā'* while a man neglects his due effort, such as repentance for sins and purification of the heart.[81]

Nonetheless, Ghazālī also teaches that at the highest stage of the Sufi way, *duᶜā’* falls off. There is, at this stage, no need for it in the strict sense of supplication.

According to Ghazālī,[82] for example, there are three stages in the state of *tawakkul* (trust in God). The first stage occurs when man's trust in God is like his trust in his guardian (*wakīl*). Trust is limited and self-conscious in this case. In the second stage, man's trust in God is like that of a little child in his mother.

> He does not know anybody but her, nor does he rely upon anybody but her. When he sees her, he stays around her all the time, and never leaves her alone. If something happens in her absence, the first word to come to his tongue is 'Mummy' and the first idea to come to his mind is his mother . . .[83]

The difference between these two stages is that in the second stage man is not conscious of his own trust in God, while in the first there is still present a self-conscious exertion (*takalluf*). In this second stage, every deliberation and calculation (*tadbīr*) on the part of man is gone, except that he takes refuge in God with *duᶜā’*, or supplication, like a little child who cries out for milk. The little child has no doubt that the mother listens to him. So the man in this second stage of *tawakkul* knows that God never fails to answer his *duᶜā’*.

In the third (and highest) stage of *tawakkul*, man's state of trust in God is that of the corpse in the hands of the washer. As he is dead to himself, his movement is entirely under the control of the eternal power of God. This state is like that of a little child who knows that his mother knows what he wants, and that she looks for him even if he does not look for her. In this final stage, *duᶜā’* disappears because of man's complete trust in God's generosity (*karam*) and care (*ᶜināya*), and because of his conviction that favours are given before request. Ghazālī describes this state as very rare. It does not usually last long, like the pale colour of horror (*ṣufrat al-wajal*) in the face; a man in this state looks dumbfounded (*mabhūt*).[84] Thus we may conclude that he means by this third *tawakkul* the ecstatic state of the Sufi.[85]

Nonetheless, Ghazālī's interest in *duʿāʾ* is more practical. He is more concerned with the benefit (*fāʾida*) of *duʿāʾ* in the Sufi way. First of all, *duʿāʾ*, or supplication, requires the presence of the heart (*ḥuḍūr al-qalb*), which is the apex of all acts of worship.[86] Man's heart usually does not turn to the remembrance of God unless there is need or suffering from calamity and misfortune. For man, as God says, *when ill luck afflicts him, is full of endless supplication* (*duʿāʾ*).[87] Need brings *duʿāʾ*, and *duʿāʾ* in turn brings the heart back to God.[88]

Duʿāʾ not only brings the heart back to the remembrance of God, but also brings back to the heart humility (*taḍarruʿ*) and submissiveness (*khushūʿ*) to God.[89] Ghazālī mentions this inner attitude as one of the ten conditions of *duʿāʾ*,[90] and he stresses the significance of this quality of humbleness on the part of man in his relation to God.[91] It is the very expression of human impotence and servanthood (*ʿubūdīya*). Man supplicates when he gives up all his will and selfish efforts, realising the limits of his power. He turns to God, the Almighty, with full trust in Him. It is, therefore, a mark of man's submissiveness (*riqqa*) to God, and at the same time it shows God's omnipotence and lordliness (*rabbānīya*).

Consequently, there is not, and should not be, any self-conscious effort suggestive of human power in *duʿāʾ*. The reason why Ghazālī dislikes the *sajʿ*-style in prayers—no matter what the real and original reason for its rejection in prayers in the Traditions may be[92]—is that he discerns in it man's presumptuous attempt to win over the will of God by means of stylistic refinement of prayers.[93] This is still a form of self-reliance, and therefore there is no purity and perfection in such a one's surrender to God.

Ghazālī adds other conditions for the inner attitude of the supplicant: longing (*raghba*), fear (*rahba*), unconditionality in supplication, and sincere hope for God's response.[94] 'Unconditionality' and 'sincere hope' express complete trust in God, and man's thinking well (*ḥusn al-ẓann*) of God. These mean the faith that God is 'powerful over everything' (*qādir ᶜalā kulli shay'*), that He never fails to respond to man's *duᶜā'*, and that He knows his interest best and is Merciful.[95]

Therefore, even if God does not apparently respond to man's *duᶜā'*, or if the result is different from what he expected, it no longer matters. God knows best what is good for him. It may be man's expectation that is wrong. So when his *duᶜā'* is fulfilled, he thanks God, saying, 'Praise be to God, by Whose grace good deeds are fulfilled!' When it is not fulfilled either soon or as expected, he also praises Him, saying, 'Praise be to God under all conditions!'[96] He has no right to complain about the outcome of *duᶜā'*, saying, 'I have prayed, but I have not been answered yet'.[97] All this is essential to the state of *tawakkul*, which is the reverse side of the true *tawḥīd*.

There seems to be some contradiction involved here when Ghazālī adds to this another condition of 'fear' (*rahba*).[98] But there is none in reality: it is exactly for the purpose of removing man's conceit (*ᶜujb*) and haughtiness (*kibr*), and of instilling in his heart gratitude to God. God will certainly answer *duᶜā'* addressed to Him. But He is under no obligation whatsoever. He is absolutely free.

Ghazālī also mentions 'longing' as another condition of the suppliant.[99] This means that man can ask for anything he wants. God is unrivalled in generosity, greatness, and mercy. There is nothing He cannot do. Therefore, man should not hesitate to make *duᶜā'* to Him even if he thinks he is unworthy of it. Ghazālī quotes the following saying of Sufyān ibn ᶜUyayna:

> Let not any of you give up supplication (*duᶜā'*) because of what he knows about himself. For God answered even the supplication (*duᶜā'*) of the worst creature, Iblīs, when

he said, *'My Lord, give me respite until the day when they are resurrected'*, and God said, *'You are among those who are given respite'*.[100]

Furthermore, G͟hazālī mentions purity of the heart and repentance for sins as other conditions of the suppliant. According to G͟hazālī, this inner purity is the direct cause of the divine response, or an occasion through which the divine response takes place according to God's Custom.[101] Therefore it does not contradict the previous condition: longing and hope in *duʿāʾ*. Real hope (*rajāʾ*) comes only after the suppliant has done all he can.[102]

All these conditions mentioned by G͟hazālī express man's self-denial, servanthood (*ʿubūdīya*), and impotence, as well as God's All-Powerfulness, Lordliness, and Majesty, and consequently man's complete surrender to and dependence on Him. It is difficult in the beginning to fulfil all these inner conditions at each *duʿāʾ*. Nevertheless, the novice can overcome this initial difficulty and thus appropriate the inner qualities expressed in those conditions by repeated practice. In so doing these qualities gradually become his second nature. Thus he converts the dogmatic teaching of *tawḥīd* into truly interiorised thought.[103] Is this not what God really means when He commands us to make *duʿāʾ* to Him? At least, this educational effect of *duʿāʾ* is what G͟hazālī means when he says:

> Supplication (*duʿāʾ*) for forgiveness, for safety against sins, and for other virtues which are to be sought from religious practices, is not contradictory to contentment (*riḍā*) with the Decree of God. For God lets His servants devote themselves to supplication so that it may produce in them undistracted remembrance (*ṣafāʾ al-d͟hikr*), submissiveness of the heart (*k͟hus͟hūʿ*), and humble docility (*riqqat al-taḍarruʿ*). Thus these may become an illumination (*jalāʾ*) and a cause for which special manifestations of divine grace (*lutf*) are granted, just as lifting a cup and

> drinking water are not contradictory to contentment with God's Decree of thirst . . .[104]

If *duᶜā'* is so vital to the inner life of the human heart, it is best to make *duᶜā'* as often as possible on every occasion in our daily lives, without waiting for need, calamity, or ill luck. Man may make supplication for future happiness both in this world and the next, as well as for deliverance from present calamity and sin. Since man is all mortal, there is enough reason for him to make *duᶜā'* at every moment.

Many beautiful prayers have been transmitted for this purpose from the Prophet, the early pious Muslims, and the saints. There are several reasons for using the transmitted prayers. The first is that they are supposed to be particularly efficacious because of their connection with special holy men or occasions. The second is that by using model prayers transmitted from the experts on *duᶜā'*, the suppliant can learn how to make *duᶜā'* in the proper manner (i.e. the external form). For, in the beginning, 'not everybody is good at making supplication (*duᶜā'*)'.[105] The third is that by using ready-made prayers man not only learns how to make supplication, but also—and this is more important—learns the inner attitude proper to his relation to God. Thus Ghazālī advises the novice to learn by heart all the important prayers[106] and to make supplication with them at every moment of his daily life.

In sum, Ghazālī's notion of *duᶜā'* is traditional in the sense that it is no more than the original Qur'ānic meaning of supplication. However, *duᶜā'* in Ghazālī's thought is more emphasized as a method and for its practical effect in the Sufi way than as *duᶜā'* as such, or 'a spontaneous manifestation of emotion'.[107]

The best way to keep remembering God is to organise and regulate daily life for this single purpose with the practices of invocation (*dhikr*), supplication (*duᶜā'*), Qur'ān-recitation (*qirā'a*), and meditation (*fikr*). Ghazālī elaborates these practices by dividing a whole day into twelve parts (*wird*), including the time for sleep. To each of these *wird*s he assigns specific exercises for the remembrance of God.[108]

There are, however, many other occasions for *dhikr* and *duʿāʾ* which require special practices different from the regular daily pattern, as on Friday[109] among the weekdays, and during Ramaḍān[110] and the Ḥajj[111] in the course of the year. Ghazālī also mentions *dhikr*-formulas and *duʿāʾ*-texts for such special occasions as travelling,[112] marriage,[113] funerals,[114] drought,[115] eclipses of the sun and the moon,[116] rain (p. 85), thunder (p. 85), wind (p. 84), physical pain (pp. 86–87), anger (p. 85), fear of people (p. 86), grief (p. 87), and others.[117] Thus every moment of daily life is punctuated by the practice of *dhikr* and *duʿāʾ*.

Notes to Introduction

1 Among many other studies on his life and thought, see D.B. Macdonald, 'The Life of al-Ghazzālī, with Especial Reference to his Religious Experiences and Opinions', *JAOS* 20 (1899), 71–132; W.M. Watt, *Muslim Intellectual: A Study of al-Ghazali*. For recent unique—though somewhat one-sided in their conclusions—attempts to understand Ghazālī's thought and behaviour in the political background, see F. Jabre, 'La biographie et l'oeuvre de Ghazālī réconsidérées à la lumière des *Ṭabaqāt* de Sobkī', *MIDEO* 1 (1954), 73–102; idem, *La notion de certitude selon Ghazali*; H. Laoust, *La politique de Ġazālī*.

2 *Al-Munqidh min al-ḍalāl*, translated by W.M. Watt in his *The Faith and Practice of al-Ghazālī*, 21.

3 To give a brief account of this important term, Ghazālī uses it in two different senses: according to logicians and theologians, it means acceptance of a certain statement because it is logically proved and free from doubt (*shakk*) or any possibility of doubt, while according to the Sufis it means acceptance of a statement not only because there is no doubt about it, whether logically proven or based on the generally accepted authority, but also because it grips the heart to such an extent that it dominates one's entire concern and there is a full commitment to it (*Iḥyā'*, I. 73 [*K. al-ᶜIlm*, bāb 6]).

4 Jabre stresses the decisive influence of Ismāᶜīlism on this inner development of Ghazālī (see his *La notion de certitude*, particularly Part III).

5 *Al-Munqidh* (tr. Watt), 56.

6 See below, xxvii–xxviii.

7 *Al-Munqidh* (tr. Watt), 59. For the disputes about the period and course of his wandering, see W.M.Watt, *Muslim Intellectual*, 144–48; A.L. Tibawi, 'Al-Ghazālī's Tract on Dogmatic Theology', *IQ* 9 (1965), 65–122.

8 This does not necessarily mean that Ghazālī lost interest in the actual problems of the Islamic Community at large as Laoust emphatically asserts in his recent work (op. cit.). One of our next problems, then, will be to investigate how Ghazālī relates the Sufi ideal and practice to the social and political problems of the Community.

9 M. Bouyges, *Essai de chronologie des oeuvres de al-Ghazālī*, ed. M. Allard, 41–44.

10 In spite of this great significance, there have been few serious attempts to analyse its contents and to solve such problems: What is the real motive behind his composition of it? How did it come to take its present form? What are the differences in form and content, if any, between the *Iḥyā'* and its summaries, *Kīmiyā' al-saᶜāda* (Persian) and *Kitāb al-arbaᶜīn fī uṣūl al-dīn*? What *genre* of Islamic literature does it belong to? etc. (Cf. W.M. Watt, *Muslim Intellectual*, 151.)

11 *Iḥyā'*, I. 305 (below, 29).

12 Needless to say, Ghazālī does not mean by the word 'heart' the physical one (*al-laḥm al-ṣanawbarī*), but something 'subtle (*laṭīfa*), lordly (*rabbānī*), and spiritual (*rūḥānī*)' (*Iḥyā'*, III. 3 [*K. ᶜAjā'ib al-qalb*, Bayān maᶜnā al-nafs]) in man, which cannot be grasped by the senses. This heart is also called 'spirit' (*rūḥ*), or 'the serene soul' (*al-nafs al-muṭma'inna*), or 'a precious substance' (*jawhar nafīs*), or 'noble pearl' (*durr ᶜazīz*) (*Iḥyā'*, I. 54 [*K. al-ᶜIlm*, bāb 5]). It is not a bodily part of man. Nonetheless, it is related to the physical heart in a way no one but a few can know. It is 'that part of man which grasps (*mudrik*), knows (*ᶜālim*), and intuits (*ᶜārif*)' (*Iḥyā'*, III. 3), namely, a continuous entity of man or the subject who thinks, perceives, and moves the body, which is its instrument and vessel. It is something that cannot be the object of thinking and perception. In short, it is 'the essence of man' (*ḥaqīqat al-insān*) (*Iḥyā'*, III. 3). See also below, 22n.

13 There is a subtle relationship between the heart and the body, and it is through the latter that man can transform and purify the heart, and thus disclose its essential nature inclined to turn to God. For instance, its essential virtue of humility can be manifested only through the bodily activities of humility.

14 Cf. Q. II:47, II:63, II:200, VII:69 etc.

15 Cf. Q. LXXXVII:15.

16 Cf. Q. II:114, XXII:40, XXIV:36–7, etc.

17 Cf. Q. XX:14.

18 Cf. Q. XXXVIII:32, LXII:9. If the central meaning of the ritual prayer is 'praise of God's greatness and power, and thanksgiving for the salvation bestowed by Him' (F. Heiler, *Das Gebet*, 444), then it is no wonder that dhikr of God as such should be the essential part of ritual prayer, or even be regarded as ritual prayer itself.

19 Generally speaking, as a religious behaviour which

originally came into being as a spontaneous response to God becomes formalised, its meritoriousness is more and more emphasized. (Cf. Heiler, 150–56, 479–85.)

20 Cf. Q. LXII:10, LXIII:9, etc.

21 For example, as a form of night vigil (Q. LXXIII:6–8, LXXVI:25).

22 For this (later) development of dhikr, see L. Gardet, 'Un problème de mystique comparée', *RT* 52 (1952), 642–79; 53 (1953), 197–216; idem, 'Dhikr', *EI*[2], II. 223–27; L. Massignon, *Essai sur les origines du lexique technique de la mystique musulmane*, 81–98; W.S. Haas, 'The Zikr of the Rahmanija-Order in Algeria: A Psycho-Physiological Analysis', *MW* 33 (1943), 16–28; T.P.Hughes, 'Zikr', *Dictionary of Islam*, 703–710.

23 *Iḥyā'*, IV. 176 (*K. al-Khawf*, Bayān maʿnā sū' al-khātima).

24 *Iḥyā'*, III. 29 (*K. ʿAjā'ib al-qalb*, Bayān tasalluṭ al-shayṭān).

25 Therefore, *dhikr* must go hand in hand with other ascetic practices such as repentance, renunciation, seclusion, poverty, and other efforts to 'transform one's whole character after the attributes of God' (*al-takhalluq bi-akhlāq Allāh*) in order to sever the attachment to the world.

26 *Iḥyā'*, I. 138–39 (*K. al-Ṭahāra*, qism 3, nawʿ 1); I. 163–64 (*K. Ṣalāt*, Bayān al-dawā' al-nāfiʿ). For meditation on death see *Iḥyā'*, *Kitāb dhikr al-mawt wa-mā baʿdahu.* (Tr. Winter, *The Remembrance of Death and the Afterlife.*)

27 See below, xxv–xxvi.

28 *Iḥyā'*, IV. 434–36 (*K. Dhikr al-mawt*, bāb 1; tr. Winter, 7–14).

29 *Iḥyā'*, IV. 412 (*K. al-Tafakkur*, Bayān ḥaqīqat al-fikr).

30 Hence Ghazālī often uses these two terms (*dhikr* and *fikr*) in combination (*Iḥyā'*, I. 194 [*K. al-Ṣalāt*, bāb 7, qism 1]; I. 334 [*K. Tartīb al-awrād*, bāb 1, Faḍīlat al-awrād] and passim).

31 For the arguments about the syntax of this formula, see E.W. Lane's *Arabic-English Lexicon*, II. 639.

32 *Iḥyā'*, I. 300 (below, 15).

33 See below, 14n.

34 *Iḥyā'*, I. 300 (below, 14).

35 Cf. *Iḥyā'*, I, 303 (below, 23–25).

36 *Iḥyā'*, I. 299 (below, 13). The *ḥadīth* is to be found in Ṭabarānī, *al-Muʿjam al-Kabīr*, no.5074; Abū Nuʿaym, IX. 254.

37 *Iḥyā'*, I. 303.

38 This is, according to Ghazālī, the reason why the Prophet Muḥammad preferred *tahlīl* for *dhikr* to the rest of the formulas (*Iḥyā'*, I. 305 [below, p.29]).

39 These four practices are called 'the Four Offices' (*al-*

waẓā'if al-arbaᶜa), which constituted the main part of the daily practices of Ghazālī. (Cf. *Iḥyā'*, I. 333–67 [*K. Tartīb al-awrād*]; Ghazālī, *Bidāyat al-hidāya* [*The Beginning of Guidance*], trans. by W.M. Watt in *The Faith and Practice*, 86–152).

40 *Iḥyā'*, I. 303 (below, 22); I. 305 (below, 29) and passim.

41 *Iḥyā'*, I. 303 (below, 23–24). Cf. *Iḥyā'*, II. 292 (*K. al-Samāᶜ*, bāb 2, maqām 2) and passim.

42 For this important term, see note A on p. 30 below.

43 *Iḥyā'*, III. 35 (*K. ᶜAjā'ib al-qalb*, Bayān tafṣīl madākhil al-shayṭān).

44 *Iḥyā'*, III. 18–19 (*K. ᶜAjā'ib al-qalb*, Bayān al-farq bayn al-ilhām . . .).

45 Strictly speaking, however, this 'will and effort' is not his own, but God's.

46 Cf. Q. XII:31.

47 *Iḥyā'*, II. 288 (*K. al-Samāᶜ*, bāb 2, maqām 1).

48 *Iḥyā'*, III. 395 (*K. Dhamm al-ghurūr*, ṣinf 3).

49 *Iḥyā'*, IV. 241 (*K. al-Tawḥīd*, Bayān ḥaqīqat al-tawḥīd).

50 *Iḥyā'*, III. 18 (*K. ᶜAjā'ib al-qalb*, Bayān al-farq . . .).

51 The vision of God is not complete in this world. It is but a foretaste of the blissful experience of seeing Him in the Hereafter. Man's worldly existence is a preparation for this supreme goal.

52 Cf. *Iḥyā'*, I. 304 (below, 26); Zabīdī, *Itḥāf*, V. 23.

53 Cf. above, n.51.

54 I have deliberately avoided the word 'prayer' in English for the Arabic word *duᶜā'*, when its meaning is thus limited, since the term 'prayer' in English and in other Christian contexts has been used in such an extended sense that it is misleading to use this term except for the text of *duᶜā'* and ritual prayer (for *ṣalāt*).

55 Tahānawī, *Kashshāf iṣṭilāḥāt al-funūn*, II. 503–4. See also, e.g., *Iḥyā'*, IV. 258 (*K. al-tawḥīd*, Bayān mā qālahu . . .).

56 For this topic, see A. Schimmel, 'Some Aspects of Mystical Prayers in Islam', *WI* 2 (1952), 112–25, cf. the comparative discussion on 'mystical prayer' in F. Heiler, *Das Gebet*.

57 Cf. Q. VI:56, XL:74, LXXII:18–20.

58 Q. XL:60.

59 Q. II:186.

60 *Iḥyā'*, I. 313–5 (below, 50–6).

61 *Iḥyā'*, I. 324–6 (below, 71–79).

62 *Iḥyā'*, I. 311–3 (below, 46–50).

63 *Iḥyā'*, I. 309–11 (below, 41–46).

64 *Iḥyā'*, I. 207 (*K. al-Ṣalāt*, bāb 7, qism 4).

65 *Iḥyā'*, I. 207–8 (ibid.).

66 See, for example, the list of manuals in C.E. Padwick, *Muslim Devotions: A Study of Prayer-Manuals in Common Use*, 289–97.

67 Heiler, 307–9.

68 Heiler, 308.

69 Qushayrī, *al-Risāla al-Qushayrīya*, II. 527.

70 See Appendix I.

71 Schimmel, 'Mystical Prayers', 112.

72 M. Smith, *Rābiʿa the Mystic*, 24.

73 Tirmidhī, Duʿā', I; quoted in *Iḥyā'*, I. 333 (below, 91).

74 Qushayrī, II. 527.

75 Ibid.

76 Schimmel, 'Mystical Prayers', 113.

77 Ibid.

78 Since *duʿā'*, or supplication, represents the 'personal' relationship between man and God, it also raises a problem among theologians. First of all, the Muʿtazilites deny its usefulness, because, in their opinion, 'it would be derogatory to the pure divine transcendence' (L. Gardet, art. 'Duʿā'', *EI*[2], II. 617–8). God's promised response to the offered *duʿā'* means no more than 'the just reward for a rationally good action that He is guaranteeing' (ibid.). On the other hand, the Ashʿarites and 'philosophers' (*falāsifa*) approve it from a different viewpoint. The Ashʿarites consider that *duʿā'* will be answered if that is the will of God, but not always as is requested. As for the 'philosophers' (e.g. Ibn Sīnā), they include *duʿā'* in their universal determinism, as 'a result of the co-operation of terrestrial disposition and celestial causes' (ibid.).

79 *Iḥyā'*, I. 333 (below, 90–91).

80 Being an Ashʿarite, Ghazāli does not admit the law of causality. Supplications, shields, and watering, etc. are 'causes' through which God removes affliction, deflects arrows, and makes plants grow; they are occasions through which the Divine Agency works. Therefore, the real cause is God Himself. But there is a kind of regularity (but not necessity) in the divine causation, called the *Sunna* of God (*sunnat Allāh*) or the Custom of God (*ʿādat Allāh*), which in practice comes very close to the idea of the laws of nature. Nonetheless, they are fundamentally different—one is meaningful and the other lacks meaning. Hence man's duty is to make preparations for the divine grace according to this *Sunna* of God. See also below, 90–91.

81 Cf. *Iḥyā'*, III. 37 (*K. ʿAjā'ib al-qalb*, Bayān tafṣīl madākhil al-shayṭān . . .). Ghazālī also mentions inner purity or repentance as one of the ten conditions for *duʿā'* (*Iḥyā'*, I. 309–11 [below, 41–46]).

82 *Iḥyā'*, IV. 255 (*K. al-Tawḥīd*, Shaṭr 2, Bayān ḥāl al-tawakkul).

83 *Iḥyā'*, IV. 255 (ibid.).

84 *Iḥyā'*, IV. 255, 256 (ibid.).

85 See above, xxvii.

86 *Iḥyā'*, I. 303 (below, 22); I. 333 (below, 91).

87 Q. XLI:51.

88 *Iḥyā'*, ibid. (below, 91).

89 *Iḥyā'*, ibid. (below, 91).

90 *Iḥyā'*, I. 308 (below, 38–9).

91 *Iḥyā'*, I. 308 (below, 37–9) and passim. Ghazālī says that the posture of prostration (*sujūd*) is particularly appropriate to receive the divine response, citing a Tradition: 'Man is nearest to God when he prostrates. So make many supplications at that time'. (Muslim, Ṣalāt, 215.) This might be interpreted to mean that prostration best expresses man's humility.

92 See below, 36, n.B.

93 *Iḥyā'*, I. 307–8 (below, 36–8).

94 See *Iḥyā'*, I. 308–9 (below, 39).

95 Zabīdī, author of the ten-volume commentary on the *Iḥyā'*, comments as follows: 'Verily the conditions of the believer are all good. The divine decree of happiness and adversity for him is mercy and favour. If the veil is removed from him, he will be more pleased with adversity than happiness. God knows best the interests of His servants'. (*Itḥāf al-sāda*, V. 40.)

96 *Iḥyā'*, I. 309 (below, 40).

97 *Iḥyā'*, I. 309 (below, 40).

98 *Iḥyā'*, I. 308 (below, 38).

99 *Iḥyā'*, I. 308 (below, 38–9).

100 *Iḥyā'*, I. 309 (below, 39). The Qur'ānic citation is from VII:14–15.

101 *Iḥyā'*, I. 309–11 (below, 68–70). See also above, n.80.

102 Cf. *Iḥyā'*, IV. 139 (*K. al-Khawf*, Bayān ḥaqīqat al-rajā').

103 Cf. above, xxiii.

104 *Iḥyā'*, IV. 343 (*K. al-Maḥabba*, Bayān anna 'l-duʿā' . . .).

105 *Iḥyā'*, I. 308 (below, 37).

106 *Iḥyā'*, I. 333 (below, 90).

107 Heiler, *Das Gebet*, 352.

108 *Iḥyā'*, I. 333–67 (*K. Tartīb al-awrād*). See also Ghazālī, *Bidāyat al-hidāya* (as translated by Montgomery Watt in his *The Faith and Practice*), 86–130.

109 *Iḥyā'*, I. 178–209 (*K. al-Ṣalāt*, bāb 5).

110 *Iḥyā'*, I. 201–203 (*K. al-Ṣalāt*, bāb 6, qism 3); 231–40 (*K. al-Ṣawm*).

111 *Iḥyā'*, I. 240–73 (*K. al-Ḥajj*).

112 *Iḥyā'*, II. 243–302 (*K. Ādāb al-safar*).

113 *Iḥyā'*, II. 21–62 (*K. al-Nikāḥ*).

114 *Iḥyā'*, I. 205 (*K. al-Ṣalāt*, bāb 6, qism 4).

115 *Iḥyā'*, I. 204–205 (ibid.).

116 *Iḥyā'*, I. 204 (ibid.).

117 See below, Ch. v.

THE BOOK OF INVOCATIONS AND SUPPLICATIONS[A]

PROLOGUE

In the name of God, Most Compassionate and Merciful

PRAISE BE TO GOD; Whose compassion is all-embracing and Whose mercy is universal; Who rewards His servants for their remembrance [*dhikr*] [of Him] with His remembrance [of them]—verily God (Exalted is He!) has said, *Remember Me, and I will remember you*;[1] He Who has induced His servants to make petition and supplication [*du^cā'*] by His command, and said, *Supplicate to Me, and I will answer you*,[2] He Who has invited the obedient and disobedient, and those who have strayed far away and those who have remained close to Him, to joy in His majestic presence, by submitting their needs and wishes, by His Word: *Verily I am near. I respond to the supplication of a suppliant when he makes it to Me*![3] Blessing be upon Muḥammad, the lord of His prophets, and upon his Family and his Companions,[4] the foremost of His chosen ones! May God grant him peace abundantly![5]

[A] As has been discussed in the Introduction, *dhakara* and its derivatives have various meanings. In the present translation I have alternated between 'to remember', 'to invoke', or 'to mention', according to context. We must bear in mind, however, that the oral aspect of its meaning ('to invoke' or 'to mention') never goes alone without the mental aspect ('to remember') in Ghazālī's thought. I have made a distinction between *du^cā'* and *ṣalāt* by translating the former as 'supplication' and the latter as 'ritual prayer', although without dogmatic consistency. I have sometimes translated *da^cawāt* (pl. of *da^cwa*) or *ad^ciya* (pl. of *du^cā'*) as 'prayers' in the sense of the formulas of supplication.

To proceed. Besides the reading of the Book of God,[A] no act of worship made by the tongue is more meritorious than the invocation [*dhikr*] of God (Exalted is He!) and submitting one's needs to Him in undistracted prayers. Therefore, there should be a general explanation of the merit of the invocation [of God] and mention of important examples of it in particular; also, an explanation of the merit of supplication, with its conditions and forms. There should be reference to some prayers which have been transmitted to serve both religious and mundane purposes, and to some which are particularly used for asking forgiveness [*su'āl al-maghfira*], refuge-taking [*isti*ᶜ*ādha*], and so forth. This discussion will be set forth in five Chapters:

Chapter One	On the Merit and Profit of Invocation: in General and in Particular.
Chapter Two	On the Merit and Forms of Supplication; the Merit of Asking for Forgiveness and of Invoking Blessing upon the Emissary of God (may God bless him and grant him peace).
Chapter Three	On Transmitted [*ma'thūra*] Prayers whose Authors and Circumstances [of Composition] are Known.

[A] The Qur'ān.

CHAPTER FOUR	On Selections from among the Transmitted Prayers, with the *Isnād*[A] Omitted.
CHAPTER FIVE	On Prayers Transmitted for every Emergent Occasion.

[A] The chain of the names of the transmitters who handed on the Prophet's word or deed.

CHAPTER ONE

On the General Merit and Profit of Invocation, with an Illustration from the Qur'ān, the Traditions, and the Narratives

From the Qur'ān:

THE general merit of invocation is testified to by the Word of God: *Remember Me, and I will remember you.*[6] Thābit al-Bunānī said, 'Verily I know when my Lord remembers me'. So the people became alarmed at him and asked, 'How do you know that?' He said, 'When I remember God, He remembers me'.

God has said, *Remember God often,*[7] and *When you rush together from* ᶜ*Arafāt*[A] *in a crowd, remember God at the Holy Monument* [al-mashᶜar al-ḥarām]*; and remember Him as He has guided you*[8] and *When you have completed your holy rites, remember God, as you remember your fathers, or more devoutly*[9] and . . . *those who remember God, standing, sitting, or lying down on their sides*[10] and *When you have performed the ritual prayer* [ṣalāt], *remember God, standing, sitting, or lying down on your sides*[11] [on which] Ibn ᶜAbbās (may God be pleased with him) commen-

[A] The plain where a halt (*wuqūf*), one of the main rites of the Pilgrimage, takes place on the ninth day (ᶜ*arafa*) of the (twelfth) month of Dhu 'l-Ḥijja. After the sunset the pilgrims rush down toward Muzdalifa and here they offer the joint sunset and evening prayer. The mosque is illuminated and all spend the night there. This place is called *al-mashᶜar al-ḥarām* in the Qur'ān (A. J. Wensinck, J. Jomier, and B. Lewis, 'Ḥadjdj', *EI*², III. 31–38).

ted, 'That is: [remember God] whether at night or during the day, whether travelling or remaining at home, whether in poverty or in riches, in sickness or in health, in private or in public'.[A]

Denouncing the hypocrites, God (Exalted is He!) has said, *They remember God but seldom.*[12] And He has said, *Remember your Lord, in your soul, with humility and fear, not with a loud voice, morning and evening. Be not among the heedless.*[13] *Truly the remembrance of God is greater.*[14] Ibn ᶜAbbās (may God show him His mercy) said, 'This has two interpretations: one is that God's remembrance of you is greater than your remembrance of Him, and the other is that the remembrance of God is greater than any other act of worship',[B] etc.

From the Traditions:[C]

The Emissary of God (may God bless him and grant him peace) said, 'An invoker of God among the heedless is like a green tree in the midst of dry stalk'.[15] He said (may God bless him and grant him peace), 'An invoker of God among the heedless is like a fighter [for the sake of God] among deserters'.[16]

He said (may God bless him and grant him peace), 'God[D]

[A] Ṭabarī, v. 154, and see also Bayḍāwī, 133. On the other hand, some commentators interpret this passage in relation to the *ṣalāt al-khawf*, i.e. 'When you perform the prayer [in time of war], remember God [and perform it] standing, sitting . . .' (Zamakhsharī, I. 560).

[B] As to this commentary and some others by Ibn ᶜAbbās, see Ṭabarī, II. 93–4.

[C] A distinction is made in this translation between the 'Traditions' (*akhbār*, pl. of *khabar*) and the 'Narratives' or the ancestral sayings (*āthār*, pl. of *athar*). The former is used for the Prophet, and the latter for the eminent pious persons of the early period of Islam.

[D] A distinction is made throughout this translation between the Qur'ānic revelation of God through Gabriel and the other type of revelation, called the 'divine Tradition' (*ḥadīth qudsī* or *ilāhī*), which is a Tradition giving the words spoken by God, by putting the former in the present perfect tense and the latter in the present tense in accordance with the text. (This is also distinguished from the Prophetic Tradition, or *ḥadīth nabawī*, which gives the words of the Prophet.) (J. Robson, 'Ḥadīth Qudsī', *EI*², III. 28–9; S.M. Zwemer, 'The So-Called Hadith Qudsi', in his *Studies in Popular Islam*, 121–34; L. Massignon, *Essai*, 120–28, 135–56.)

says, "I am with My servant so long as he invokes Me and his lips move for invoking Me" '.[17]

He said, 'No act of a human being is so efficacious for deliverance from God's punishment as the invocation of God (Great and Glorious is He!)'. The people asked, 'O Emissary of God. Nor is the *jihād* for the sake of God so efficacious [as the invocation of God]?' He said, 'No, no *jihād* for the sake of God is so efficacious, except that you hit with your sword until it is intercepted and then you hit with it again until it is intercepted, and then you hit with it until it is intercepted, [while remembering God]'.[18]

He said (may God bless him and grant him peace), 'Let him who wishes to graze[19] in the pastures of the Garden invoke God constantly'.[20]

On being asked, 'Which act is most meritorious?' the Emissary of God (may God bless him and grant him peace) said, '[It is] that you die while your tongue is moistened with the invocation of God (Great and Glorious is He!)'.[21]

He said, 'Let your tongue be moistened with the invocation of God morning and evening, and then no fault will fall upon you'.[22]

He said (may God bless him and grant him peace), 'Truly the invocation of God (Great and Glorious is He!) morning and evening is more meritorious than breaking swords for the sake of God and giving wealth lavishly'.[23]

He said (may God bless him and grant him peace), 'God (Blessed and Exalted is He!) says, "When My servant remembers Me in his heart, I remember him in My heart. When he remembers Me in company [with others], I remember him in an even better company. When he draws near to Me a hand's breadth, I draw near to him an arm's length. When he draws near to Me an arm's length, I draw near to him a fathom. When he draws near to Me walking, I draw near to him running" '[24]—meaning by 'running' one's quickness of response.

He said (may God bless him and grant him peace), 'God (Great and Glorious is He!) spreads His shade upon seven people on the Day when there is no shade but His.[A] Among them is a man[25] who invoked God privately and whose eyes overflowed [with tears] from the fear of God'.[26]

Abu'l-Dardā' said, 'The Emissary of God (may God bless him and grant him peace) said, "Shall I not tell you about the best and purest of your works for your Lord, and the most exalted of them in your ranks, and the work which is better for you than giving silver and gold, and better for you than encountering your enemy, with you striking their necks and them striking your necks?" Thereupon the people said, "What is that, O Emissary of God?" He said, "The constant remembrance of God" '.[27]

The Emissary of God said, 'God (Great and Glorious is He!) says, "He who is so occupied with the remembrance of Me that he does not make petition to Me, I will give him the best of what I give to suppliants" '.[B] [28]

From the Narratives:

Al-Fuḍayl said, 'We are told that God says, "O My servant![29] Remember Me for an hour after the morning prayer [*ṣubḥ*][30] and for an hour after the afternoon prayer [*ᶜaṣr*], then I will preserve you [from sins] during the interval between the two" '.

One of the learned said, 'God (Great and Glorious is He!) says, "Whoever a man may be, if I have examined his heart and found it dominated by the constant practice of remembrance of Me, I will manage his affairs and be his companion, his partner in conversation and his intimate friend" '.

[A] On the Day of Resurrection.

[B] Cf. Kalābādhī's comment on this Tradition in his *Taᶜarruf* (translated by Arberry as *The Doctrine of the Sufis*, 106).

Al-Ḥasan said, 'Invocation is of two types: one is the invocation of God which takes place between your soul and Him. How good it is and how great its reward is! However, more meritorious than this is the invocation of God (Glorious is He!) on the occasions sanctified by Him'.

It is related that every soul departs thirsty from this world except him who remembers God.

Muᶜādh ibn Jabal (may God be pleased with him) said, 'The people of Paradise[31] never worry about anything except the time which they spent not remembering God'.

But God (Exalted is He!) knows best.[32]

The Merit of Gathering for Invocation

The Emissary of God (may God bless him and grant him peace) said, 'Whenever people sit in a gathering invoking God, the angels welcome them, and grace descends upon them, and God mentions their names to those who are beside Him'.[A] [33]

He said (may God bless him and grant him peace), 'There are no people who gather invoking God (Exalted is He!) and thereby desire nothing but His Face, without a herald from heaven calling upon them, "Rise up, O forgiven ones! Your sins have already been replaced with good deeds" '.[34]

He also said (may God bless him and grant him peace), 'Those who sit in the assembly with no invocation of God (Glorious and Exalted is He!) and no calling for blessing upon the Prophet[35]—they will all grieve on the Day of Resurrection'.[36]

David (upon whom be peace) said, 'My Lord! If You find me leaving the gatherings of rememberers [of God] for those of the heedless [of Him], then break my legs before I reach them. For that would be a grace which You could bestow upon me'.

[A] That is, the angels. Cf. Q. XXI:19–20; see also note A on p. 38 below.

The Emissary of God (may God bless him and grant him peace) said, 'The pious assembly atones for two million evil assemblies on behalf of the believers'.[37]

Abū Hurayra (may God be pleased with him) said, 'Truly the people of heaven gaze down at the houses of the people on the earth where the name of God is being invoked, just as the stars gaze down'.

Sufyān ibn ᶜUyayna said, 'When people gather to invoke God, Satan and the World retreat. Satan says to the World, "Don't you see what they are doing?" The World says, "Leave them alone. For when they are dispersed, I will catch them by the neck and bring them to you" '.

A story about Abū Hurayra. He once went to the bazaar and said, 'I see you here, while the legacy of the Emissary of God (may God bless him and grant him peace) is being distributed in the mosque'. So the people went to the mosque, deserting the bazaar. But they did not see any legacy and said, 'O Abū Hurayra! We did not see any legacy being distributed in the mosque'. He said, 'What did you see, then?' They said, 'We saw people invoking God and reciting the Qur'ān'. He said, 'That is the legacy of the Emissary of God'.[38]

Al-Aᶜmash related, on the authority of Abū Ṣāliḥ, who heard from Abū Hurayra and Abū Saᶜīd al-Khudrī, who heard the Prophet (may God bless him and grant him peace) saying, 'Verily, God (Great and Glorious is He!) has angels hovering over the earth, besides the recording angels for men [*kuttāb al-nās*].[A] When they find people invoking God, they call out to one another, "Now, come to the object of your search!" And the [other] angels come and surround them and go up to heaven. And God says, "What did you leave My servants

[A] It is believed that every man has two recording angels, one on the right side to record his good deeds and the other on the left side to record his evil deeds. As these angels are said to change every day, they are called the *muᶜaqqibāt*, or 'those who succeed each other'. (Hughes, *Dictionary*, 279. Cf. Q. LXXXII:10–11.)

doing?"[39] They reply, "We left them praising You, glorifying You and saying, 'Glory be to God!' " Thereupon God asks, "Have they seen Me?" "No", they say. Then He says, "How would it be, if they saw Me?" They say, "If they saw You, their praise, extolling and glorification would be much strengthened". He asks them, "From what do they seek protection?" "From the Fire", they reply. He asks, "Have they seen it?" "No", they say. God asks, "How would it be, if they saw it?" They reply, "If they saw it, they would be more anxious to flee from it and to shun it". God asks, "What are they seeking?" "Paradise", they say. God asks, "Have they seen it?" "No", they reply. God asks, "How would it be if they saw it?" They reply, "If they saw it, they would be more desirous of it". God says, "Verily I testify to you that I have already forgiven them". They say, "Among them is So-and-so, who did not want them, but has come only out of a particular necessity". God says, "They are such people that he who sits with them is not unhappy" '.[40]

The Merit of Tahlīl[A]

The Emissary of God (may God bless him and grant him peace) said, 'The most meritorious thing that I and the previous prophets taught is the formula: "There is no god but God, Who is alone and has no associate" '.[41]

He said (may God bless him and grant him peace), 'If someone professes a hundred times every day, "There is no god but God, Who is alone; to Him belongs sovereignty and to Him belongs praise; He is powerful over everything", then he has as good as ransomed ten slaves, and a hundred good deeds are written down for him and a hundred evil deeds are erased from him, and this formula becomes a protection for

[A] That is, to pronounce the formula: 'There is no god but God' (*lā ilāha illa 'Llāh*).

him against Satan on that day, so that no one can bring a more meritorious deed than he did except by increasing the same act more than that'.[42]

He said (may God bless him and grant him peace), 'Whenever a man performs the ritual ablution, and does it well, and raises his eyes up toward heaven, and says, "I bear witness that there is no god but God, Who is alone and has no associate, and I bear witness that Muḥammad is His servant and Emissary", then the eight[43] doors of Paradise are opened for him and he can enter through whichever one he likes'.[44]

He said (may God bless him and grant him peace), 'The people of the formula: "There is no god but God" feel lonely neither in their graves nor at their resurrection. It is as if I saw them shaking the dust off their hands at the blast [of the trumpet][A] and saying, *"Praise be to God, Who has dispelled grief from us! Verily our Lord is all-forgiving and all-thankful"* '.[45]

He also said (may God bless him and grant him peace) to Abū Hurayra, 'O Abū Hurayra, verily every good deed you perform shall be weighed on the Day of Resurrection except the testimony that "There is no god but God", as it cannot be weighed in the balance. For were it to be put on the balance of him who has confessed that formula sincerely, then even the seven heavens, the seven earths[46] and what is on them could not counterbalance on the scales the weight of the formula "There is no god but God" '.[47]

He said (may God bless him and grant him peace), 'If he who truly professes the formula: "There is no god but God" commits sins equal to the amount of the earth, God will forgive these'.[48]

He said (may God bless him and grant him peace), 'O Abū Hurayra, prompt the dead to utter the testimony: "There is no

[A] On the Day of Judgement, the Angel Isrāfīl will blow the Trump, whose sound is so loud that all men are awakened and aroused from their graves for the Judgement (Zabīdī, v. 10; Ghazālī, *The Remembrance of Death*, tr. Winter, 175–6; cf. also A.J. Wensinck, 'Isrāfīl', *SEI*, 184.)

god but God", for it utterly destroys sins'. I [Abū Hurayra] said, 'O Emissary of God, if this happens with the dead, what about the living?' He said, 'It is more effective, more effective'.[49]

He said (may God bless him and grant him peace), 'He who professes single-heartedly "There is no god but God" will enter into Heaven'.[50]

He said (may God bless him and grant him peace), 'Verily all of you will enter Paradise except him who refuses and flees from God (Great and Glorious is He!) as a camel does[51] from the camel-driver'. On being asked, 'O Emissary of God. Who is he that refuses and flees from[52] God?' he said, 'He who does not profess "There is no god but God".[53] So repeat "There is no god but God" abundantly before you become unable to do so. Verily it is the word of the profession of the unity [of God], and it is the word of the *Ikhlāṣ*[A] and it is the word of God-fearing [*kalimat al-taqwā*],[54] and it is the good word, and it is proclamation of the Truth, and it is the most firm handhold [*al-ᶜurwat al-wuthqā*],[55] and it is the price of Paradise [*thaman al-janna*]'.[56]

God (Great and Glorious is He!) has said, *Is there any reward for good except good?*[57] and it is said that 'good' in this world is the saying of the formula: 'There is no god but God' and in the Afterlife it is Paradise.[B] Hence His word: *For those that do good shall be the greatest good, and even more.*[58]

Al-Barā' ibn ᶜĀzib related that [the Prophet] said, 'If one says ten times, "There is no god but God, Who is alone; He has no associate; to Him belongs sovereignty and to Him belongs

[A] This is the title of the famous short Sura CXII, which expresses succinctly the idea of the unity of God and is, therefore, used most frequently next to the *Fātiḥa*, the opening chapter of the Qur'ān. As to its meaning, see note A on p.30 below.

[B] However, most commentators do not take the first 'good' [*al-iḥsān*] as meaning specifically *tahlīl*, but rather a good deed in general. (Zamakhsharī, IV. 49; Bayḍāwī, 549; *Jalālayn*, 495.)

praise; He is powerful over everything", then one has as good as ransomed a slave'. (Or, he said, a 'person'.)[59]

ᶜAmr ibn Shuᶜayb related, on the authority of his father,[A] who heard from his grandfather,[B] that he said that the Emissary of God (may God bless him and grant him peace) said,[60] 'If one says two hundred times a day, "There is no god but God, Who is alone; He has no associate; to Him belongs sovereignty and to Him belongs praise; He is powerful over everything", then no-one who precedes him shall supersede him, and no one who comes after him shall catch him up, except the one who does more meritorious deeds than his'.[61]

The Emissary of God (may God bless him and grant him peace) said,[62] 'If someone says in a bazaar, "There is no god but God, Who is alone; He has no associate; to Him belongs sovereignty and to Him belongs praise; He gives death and life; He is powerful over everything", then God will write for him one million good deeds and erase one million evil deeds from him, and build a mansion for him in Paradise'.[63]

It is related, 'When a man says, "There is no god but God", the word comes on the leaf [of his book],[C] and passes by [the records of his] sin, erasing them, until it finds a good deed similar to itself and then finally nestles down beside it'.

In the *Ṣaḥīḥ*,[64] there is a tradition transmitted by Abū Ayyūb, who heard the Prophet (may God bless him and grant him peace) saying, 'He who says ten times, "There is no god but God, Who is alone; He has no associate; to Him belongs sovereignty and to Him belongs praise; He is powerful over everything" is like a man who has set free four sons of Ishmael'.

[A] Shuᶜayb ibn Muḥammad, for whom see Appendix I.

[B] ᶜAbd Allāh ibn ᶜAmr ibn al-ᶜĀṣ (see Appendix I under 'Abū Muḥammad').

[C] That is, the book in which each man's deeds are recorded and which will be handed down and shown to him on the Day of Judgement (Cf. Q. LXXXIII:7–9, 18–19; LXXXIV:7–12).

There is also a Tradition in the *Ṣaḥīḥ*,[65] transmitted on the authority of ʿUbāda ibn al-Ṣāmit, that the Emissary of God (may God bless him and grant him peace) said, 'When a man wakes up at night and recites, "There is no god but God, Who is alone; He has no associate; to Him belongs sovereignty and to Him belongs praise; He is powerful over everything; Glory be to God! Praise be to God! There is no god but God; God is most great; there is no might and no power save in Him, the Exalted, the Magnificent" and says, "O God, forgive me", then God will forgive him. Or if he prays to God, he will be answered. If he performs ablution and offers ritual prayer, then his prayer will be accepted'.[66]

The Merit of Tasbīḥ,[A] Taḥmīd,[B] *and Other Invocations*

The Emissary of God (may God bless him and grant him peace) said, 'If a man says, "Glory be to God!" after ritual prayer thirty-three times and says, "Praise be to God!" thirty-three times and says, "God is most great"[C] thirty-three times and finishes the hundredth with the formula: "There is no god but God, Who is alone; He has no associate; to Him belongs sovereignty and to Him belongs praise; He is powerful over everything", then his sins are forgiven, even though they be like the foam of the sea'.[67]

He said (may God bless him and grant him peace), 'If one says, "Glory be to God, and praise be to Him!"[D] a hundred times a day, his sins fall off from him, even though they be like the foam of the sea'.[68]

It is related: A man came to the Emissary of God (may God bless him and grant him peace) and said, 'The world has turned

[A] *Subḥān Allāh*. See Appendix II.

[B] *al-Ḥamdu li'Llāh*. See Appendix II.

[C] *Allāhu akbar*. See Appendix II.

[D] *subḥān Allāh wa-bi-ḥamdih*. For the arguments about the syntax of this formula, see Lane, 639.

away from me and my wealth has become small'. The Emissary of God (may God bless him and grant him peace) said, 'How far you are from the prayer of the angels and the praise of creatures, on account of which they are supported [by God]!' So he asked,[69] 'What is that,[70] O Emissary of God?' He replied, 'Say, "Glory be to God, and praise be to Him! Glory be to God, the Magnificent![A] I beseech God for forgiveness"[B] a hundred times from the beginning of dawn until you perform the morning prayer. Then the world will come back to you, obediently and despisedly. God creates from each word an angel who praises Him with the formula: "Glory be to God!" until the Day of Resurrection, and you receive his reward'.[71]

The Emissary of God (may God bless him and grant him peace) said, 'If a servant says, "Praise be to God!" the word will fill up the space between heaven and earth. If he says, "Praise be to God!" for the second time, it will fill up the space between the seventh heaven and the lowest[72] earth. If he says, "Praise be to God!" for the third time, God (Great and Glorious is He!) will say, "Ask, and it shall be given to you"'.[73]

Rifāᶜa al-Zarqī said, 'One day we were performing the ritual prayer behind the Emissary of God (may God bless him and grant him peace). When he raised his head from bowing [*rukūᶜ*] and said, "God hearkens to him who praises Him"[C] a man behind him said, "Our Lord. Praise be to You; full, excellent, and blessed praise!" When the Emissary of God completed his ritual prayer, he asked, "Who is it that spoke before?" and the man said, "It was I, O Emissary of God". The Emissary of God said, "I saw more than thirty angels, rushing toward it, vying with one another as to who should record it first[74]"'.[75]

[A] Ar. *subḥān Allāh al-ᶜaẓīm*.

[B] Ar. *astaghfiru 'Llāh*.

[C] Ar. *samiᶜ Allāh li-man ḥamidah*. This pronouncement, called *tasmīᶜ*, has become one of the elements of the ritual prayer, together with the following *taḥmīd*: *Rabbanā wa-laka al-ḥamd ḥamd[an] kathīr[an]*.

The Emissary of God (may God bless him and grant him peace) said, 'The everlasting good deeds [*al-bāqiyāt al-ṣāliḥāt*] are the formulas: "There is no god but God. Glory be to God! Praise be to God! God is most great. There is no might and no power save in God[A]" '.[76]

He said (may God bless him and grant him peace), 'No one on earth can say, "There is no god but God. God is most great. Glory be to God! There is no might and no power save in God" without his sins being forgiven, even though they be like the foam of the sea'. This was related by Ibn ᶜUmar.[77]

Al-Nuᶜmān ibn Bas͟hīr related that the Emissary of God (may God bless him and grant him peace) said, 'Those who praise the majesty of God; glorify Him with the word: "Glory be to God!"; magnify Him with the word: "God is most great!"; and praise Him with the word: "Praise be to God!"—their words become attached around the Throne [of God] and keep praising their master with a voice[78] like the sound of bees. Who among you does not want his words of invocation to remain with God?'[79]

Abū Hurayra related that the Emissary of God (may God bless him and grant him peace) said, 'Verily my invocation of "Glory be to God! There is no god but God. God is most great" is more pleasant to me than anything else under the sun'.[80] In another version the Emissary of God added, 'There is no might and no power save in God' and said, 'These formulas are better than the world and what is in it'.

[A] Ar. *lā ḥawla wa-lā quwwata illā bi'Llāh*. There are some other interpretations of the word *ḥawl*. One of them is 'motion'. Thus the meaning of the phrase would be: 'There is no motion and no power, or ability, but by the will of God'. This is also G͟hazālī's interpretation (*Iḥyā'*, IV. 254 [*K. al-Tawḥīd*, Bayān ḥāl al-tawakkul]). The other meanings are 'changing' and 'craftiness' (Lane, 675–6; Ibn Manẓūr, XI. 189). The Qur'ān has only the form *lā quwwata illā bi'Llāh* (XVIII:39), which means, according to Bayḍāwī, the acknowledgement of impotence on the part of man and power on the part of God (Bayḍāwī, 325).

The Emissary of God (may God bless him and grant him peace) said, 'The words which are loved most by God are four: "Glory be to God!"; "Praise be to God!"; "There is no god but God"; and "God is most great". There is no harm to you, whichever of them you may mention first'. This was related by Samura ibn Jundub.[81]

Abū Mālik al-Ashᶜarī related that the Emissary of God (may God bless him and grant him peace) used to say, 'Purification is one half of belief. "Praise be to God!" will fill the scales. "Glory be to God!" and "God is most great" fill what is between heaven and earth. Ritual prayer is a light. Almsgiving is a proof. Patience is illumination. The Qur'ān is a witness for or against you. In the morning everyone becomes either a seller of his soul and a ruiner of it, or a buyer and an emancipator of it'.[82]

Abū Hurayra (may God be pleased with him) related that the Emissary of God (may God bless him and grant him peace) said, 'Two formulas are light on the tongue but heavy in the scales, and loved by the Merciful [they are]: "Glory be to God, and praise be to Him!" and "Glory be to God, the Magnificent!" '[83]

Abū Dharr (may God be pleased with him) said, 'I asked the Emissary of God (may God bless him and grant him peace), "Which word is loved most by God?" He replied, "What God has chosen for His angels, that is: Glory be to God, and praise be to Him! Glory be to God, the Magnificent!" '[84]

Abū Hurayra related that the Emissary of God (may God bless him and grant him peace) said, 'Verily God (Exalted is He!) has chosen from among the words the formulas: "Glory be to God! Praise be to God! There is no god but God. God is most great". If a man says, "Glory be to God!" twenty good deeds are written down for him and twenty evil deeds fall away from him. If he says, "God is most great" the same thing occurs'. The Prophet mentioned the same merit up to the last of the formulas.[85]

Jābir said that the Emissary of God (may God bless him and grant him peace) said, 'On behalf of him who says, "Glory be to God, and praise be to Him!" is planted a palm tree in Paradise'.[86]

According to Abū Dharr (may God be pleased with him), the poor men [*fuqarā'*][A] once said to the Emissary of God (may God bless him and grant him peace), 'The rich people take the rewards [of God] by performing ritual prayer as we do, fasting as we do, but giving the surplus of their possessions as alms'. He said, 'Didn't God already make for you that which you would give as alms? Verily you have alms to offer in each *tasbīḥ*, in each *taḥmīd*, in each *takbīr*, in each commanding of a good deed and in each prohibition of an evil deed. One of you puts a morsel in the mouth of his wife, and this is for him a form of almsgiving. There is alms even in the vulva of any of you'. The poor men said, 'O Emissary of God, shall one of us have a reward even when he submits to passion?' The Emissary of God said, 'Do you see that if he uses it for a thing forbidden, he commits a sin in it?' They said, 'Yes'. He said, 'Thus if he uses it for a thing permitted, he receives a reward in it'.[87]

Abū Dharr said, 'I said to the Emissary of God (may God bless him and grant him peace), "The people of wealth have taken away the rewards [of God]. They say what we say, but they spend, while we cannot". The Prophet said, "Shall I not show you a deed which, when you do it, you will reach [the rank of] your predecessors and supersede your successors, except those who utter the same words as yours? You say, 'Glory be to God!' thirty-three times after each ritual prayer,

[A] Among those who emigrated to Medina, leaving their homes and possessions, and settled with the Prophet, there was a group of people who were very poor (cf. Q. LIX:8; II:273). They are called the *ahl al-ṣuffa*, or the 'People of the Veranda' (where they were lodged), and are particularly respected by the later Sufis as the embodiment of poverty (*faqr*), one of the Sufi virtues (W.M. Watt, art. 'Ahl al-Ṣuffa', *EI*², I. 266–7; Hujwīrī, 19).

and 'Praise be to God!' thirty-three times, and 'God is most great!' thirty-four times" '.[88]

Yusayra[89] related that the Prophet (may God bless him and grant him peace) said, '*Tasbīḥ*, *tahlīl*, and *taqdīs* are obligatory upon you women. Never be heedless. Count with your fingers, for they will be interrogated'[90]—i.e. as witnesses at the Resurrection. Ibn ᶜUmar said, 'I saw the Prophet counting each *tasbīḥ* [with his fingers]'.[91]

The Emissary of God (may God bless him and grant him peace) said, while Abū Hurayra and Abū Saᶜīd al-Khudrī were witnessing,[92] 'When a man says, "There is no god but God" and "God is most great!" God says, "My servant has spoken the truth. There is no god but Me; I am most great!" When the man says, "There is no god but God, Who is alone; He has no associate!" God says, "My servant has spoken the truth. There is no god but Me, I am alone; I have no associate!" When the man says, "There is no god but God!" and "There is no might and no power save in God!" God says, "My servant has spoken the truth. There is no might and no power save in Me!" He who has recited these formulas on his deathbed shall never be touched by Hell'.[93]

Muṣᶜab ibn Saᶜd related on the authority of his father[A] that the Emissary of God said, 'Can any of you not earn a thousand good deeds every day?' On being asked, 'How can it be done, O Emissary of God?' he said, 'Praise God with the word "Glory be to God!" a hundred times, and a thousand good deeds will be written for you and a thousand evil deeds will fall off from you'.[94]

The Emissary of God (may God bless him and grant him peace) said, 'O ᶜAbd Allāh ibn Qays' or 'O Abū Mūsā! Shall I not show you one of the treasures of Paradise?' 'Yes', he replied. The Emissary of God said, 'Say,[95] "There is no might and no power save in God!" '[96] In another Tradition: 'Shall I

[A] Saᶜd ibn Abī Waqqāṣ.

not teach you a word from the treasury [kept] under the Throne [of God]? [It is] the formula: "There is no might and no power save in God!" '[97]

Abū Hurayra said that the Emissary of God (may God bless him and grant him peace) said, 'Shall I not show[98] you a deed which is one of the treasures of Paradise from below the Throne [of God]? [It is] the formula: "There is no might and no power save in God!" [Then] God will say, "My servant has become a Muslim and surrendered himself [to the will of God]" '.[99]

The Emissary of God (may God bless him and grant him peace) said, 'If a man says every morning, "I am content [*raḍītu*] with God as my Lord, Islam as my Religion, the Qur'ān as my Guide, and Muḥammad (may God bless him and grant him peace) as my Prophet and Emissary",[100] then God must give him contentment on the Day of Resurrection'.[101] In another tradition, 'With him who says this, God is well pleased'.[102]

Mujāhid said, 'When a man goes out of his house and says, "In the name of God!"[A] the angel says, "I guide him". When the man says, "I trust in God!" the angel says "I protect him". When the man says, "There is no might and no power save in God" the angel says, "I guard him". So the devils are dispersed away from him, and say [to their fellow devils], "What would you seek from a man who is guided, protected, and guarded? There is no way for you to approach him[103]" '.[104]

If you say: Why is it that the invocation of God, in spite of its lightness on the tongue and the little trouble involved in making it, has become more meritorious and profitable than any other act of worship in spite of the enormous hardship in them?—then you should know that the investigation of this problem is proper only to the science of unveiling [*ᶜilm al-*

[A] Ar. *bismi'Llāh*. As to this phrase, see Goldziher, 'Bismillāh', *ERE*, 666–68; Padwick, 94–101; Bayḍāwī, 2–3; *Iḥyā'*, I. 168 (*K. al-Ṣalāt*, [Bayān tafṣīl mā . . .]).

mukāshafa].[A] The extent to which it is allowed to be mentioned in the science of religious practices [*ᶜilm al-muᶜāmala*] is this: the effective and useful factor is constant invocation with the presence of the heart [*qalb*][B]. As for the invocation on the tongue and without the presence of the heart, it is of little use. There are also Traditions which confirm this point.[C] The presence of the heart at one moment in invocation, followed by heedlessness of God, because of occupation with worldly things, is also of little value. Rather the presence of heart with God, constantly or most of the time, is the preface to the acts of worship. Nay, therein is the sanctification of the rest of worship. It is the final fruition of the practical act of worship.

[A] The science of unveiling, according to Ghazālī, is the real, personal, and intuitive knowledge (*maᶜrifa*) of the essence of God, His attributes, His acts, and all other mysteries of prophecy, creation, the next world, and so forth. This knowledge is disclosed, by the grace of God, only when the human heart is completely cleansed and purified from evil qualities and detached from anything other than God. On the other hand, the practical knowledge of how to purify the heart and make it ready to receive that real knowledge is the science of religious practices. This includes the knowledge of the nature of the heart and its training as well as that of the *Sharīᶜa*. In fact, the whole *Iḥyā'* is devoted to the science of religious practices. It is a systematic and psychological analysis of human nature and a practical description of the method to train and prepare the heart for that real knowledge. And, therefore, Ghazālī always, in the *Iḥyā'*, cautiously refuses to talk about the ultimate knowledge itself from *within* and to launch into metaphysical discourse by making this kind of oblique remark (*Iḥyā'*, I. 5 [Khuṭba]; 20–21 [*K. al-ᶜIlm*, bayān ᶜilm . . . farḍ kifāya]; IV. 241 [*K. al-Tawḥīd*, Bayān ḥaqīqat al-tawḥīd], and passim).

[B] The English word 'heart' is rather associated with the emotional aspect of man. On the other hand, the Arabic word *qalb* is used by Ghazālī, as well as most Sufis, to denote the intellectual and cognitive aspects, or the essence of man (*ḥaqīqat al-insān*) and its locus. Accordingly, this concept occupies the central position in his thought (see above, xx; *Iḥyā'*, III. 2–47 [*K. ᶜAjā'ib al-qalb*]; Macdonald, *Religious Attitude*, 220–51).

[C] Zabīdī quotes a Tradition on the authority of Abū Hurayra: 'Know that God does not accept supplication from him whose heart is absent'. (Zabīdī, V. 20; Tirmidhī, Daᶜawāt, 65. See also below, 39.)

Invocation has both a beginning and an end. The beginning of it requires 'intimacy' [*uns*] and 'love' [*ḥubb*], and the end of it is required by intimacy and love,[105] and is produced by these. The aim [of invocation] is[106] this [latter] intimacy and love.[A] In the beginning the novice sometimes exerts himself to turn his heart and tongue away from the insinuation [of Satan] to the invocation of God (Great and Glorious is He!). If he is successful in persevering [in it], he obtains intimacy with invocation, and love for the One invoked is implanted in his heart.

One need not be amazed about this, for the following is the sight usually witnessed: you mention[107] before somebody a person who is not present here, and continue to mention his qualities to this person. Then he may come to love him and sometimes becomes passionately fond of the description and its frequent mention. And even if he loves to repeat the [constrained] mentioning at first, he becomes, in the end, compelled to mention it repeatedly, since he cannot refrain from it.

Truly when a man loves a thing, he repeatedly mentions it, and when he repeatedly mentions a thing, even if that may be burdensome,[108] he loves it. Thus the beginning of invocation is burdensome, until intimacy and love of the One Invoked result. And then finally it becomes impossible to endure without invocation. The cause turns into an effect and the fruit becomes fructified. This is the meaning of the saying of a man:

[A] Intimacy (with what is invoked) and love of it in the former case are accompanied by efforts (or rather, it might be said, they are the very efforts) to remain intimate and to love. On the other hand, those in the latter case are not thus accompanied—they are something agreeable and pleasant to nature, and so they need no efforts. The latter type of intimacy and love are the means (*wasīla*) to reach the *dhikr al-sirr*, where there is no presence of the human heart with anything but the Truth (Zabīdī, v. 20). Although Ghazālī does not use such terms as *dhikr al-rūḥ* and *dhikr al-sirr*, this is what is meant in this and in the following passages.

'I struggled with the reading of the Qur'ān for twenty years and I enjoyed it for twenty years'.

Enjoyment [*tanaᶜᶜum*] does not result except from intimacy and love. Intimacy results only from perseverance in endurance and effort for a long time until the effort becomes second nature. How could this be possible? Man often makes an effort to obtain food which he finds repugnant in the beginning, and then he eats it with effort and continues in that effort, after which it becomes agreeable to his nature, and finally he becomes unable to endure without it. For the soul is accustomed to, and capable of tolerating, that which you take in. 'Verily the soul becomes accustomed to what you accustom it to.'[109] That is to say: what you at first burden the soul with becomes natural to it in the end.

So if intimacy with the invocation of God (Glorious is He!) takes place, man is severed from anything else but the invocation of God and from what is other than Him. This latter is what departs from him at death and never remains with him in the grave, i.e. people, wealth, children, and political power. Nothing remains but the invocation of God. If he has already become intimate with the invocation of God (Great and Glorious is He!), he enjoys it and takes pleasure in removing the obstacles which distract it, for the needs of the mundane life hamper the invocation of God. On the other hand, no obstacle remains after death; it is as if he were alone with his beloved (and how great is his bliss!), or as if he were freed from the prison where he was hindered from what he was intimate with. Therefore, the Prophet said, 'Verily the Holy Spirit [*al-rūḥ al-qudus*] inspired in my heart: "Love anything you like. Verily you will part from it"'.[110] He meant by 'it' anything which is connected with the world.[A] For it perishes on the death [of a man], as far as he is concerned. *All that dwells upon*

[A] For the complete Tradition, see *Iḥyā'*, I. 88 (*K. al-ᶜIlm*, Bayān al-ᶜaql) and Zabīdī, I. 467.

the earth is perishing, yet still abides the Face of your Lord, the Majestic, the Generous.[111] The world perishes on his death only with regard to him, and finally it perishes in itself on the advent of its appointed time in the Book. Man enjoys this intimacy after his death until he comes close to God (Great and Glorious is He!) and rises from invocation [*dhikr*] to the Meeting [*liqā'*].[A] This takes place after what is in the graves is turned and what is in the breasts is brought out.[B] Hence it is undeniable that the invocation of God remains with him after death.

One may ask, 'Man is most likely to perish, so why is it that the invocation of God remains with him?' [We reply:] he does not come to such a kind of non-existence that prevents invocation. It is non-existence from the terrestrial and visible world [*ᶜālam al-mulk wa'l-shahāda*],[C] not from the world of the Kingdom [*ᶜālam al-malakūt*].

What we have mentioned is indicated by the word of the Emissary of God (may God bless him and grant him peace): 'The grave is either one of the pits of Hell or one of the meadows of Heaven',[D] [112] and his word: 'The spirits of the

[A] The word 'rises' (*yataraqqā*) is used only because invocation as a guide (*dalīl*) becomes a veil over what is invoked in the final stage. When a guide has shown you to the destination (*madlūl*) and you have reached what you are guided to, the role of the guide is over. So is invocation. Once you are with what is invoked there is no need for it. This is the Meeting with God (Zabīdī, v. 23).

[B] That is, the selfish intentions (*nīyāt*) and desires (*himam*). Man always stands with his intention and desire (Zabīdī, v. 23). Zabīdī rather tends to stress the psychological aspect of mystical experience. However, it must be borne in mind that Ghazālī's thought, characteristically enough, has always two aspects—psychological, and cosmological or eschatological. This passage, together with the previous one, apparently refers to the events of the Day of Resurrection as well (Cf. Q. c:9–10).

[C] See Footnote C on p.26.

[D] For the life in the grave before the Resurrection, see Ghazālī, *The Remembrance of Death*, tr. Winter, 121–148.

martyrs are in the crops of green birds',[A] [113] and by his word about the slain polytheists at Badr:[B] 'O So-and-so! O So-and-so!'—the Prophet (may God bless him and grant him peace) called the names—'Did you find what your Lord promised you to be true? Verily I found what my Lord had promised me

[A] *ṭuyūr khuḍr* (Z: *ṭayr khuḍr*). They are under the Throne of God in Paradise and go wherever they will in its gardens early and late. The same is also said about the spirits of the believers in general (see below and *Iḥyā'*, IV. 172 [*K. al-Khawf*, Bayān maʿnā sū' al-khātima]; IV. 481 [*K. Dhikr al-mawt*, Bayān ḥaqīqat al-mawt; tr. Winter, 129, 131]). For a more detailed discussion about this relationship between the human spirits and (green) birds, see Goldziher's article 'L'oiseau représentant l'âme dans les croyances populaires des musulmans', in Bousquet, ed. *Études*, [77]-[80].

[B] This battle took place in 2 AH.

[C] [Refers to p. 25] In Ghazālī's cosmology, the *ʿālam al-mulk wa'l-shahāda*, which literally means the World of Kingship and Phenomenon, is the world which is perceived by the senses. On the other hand, the *ʿālam al-malakūt*, which literally means the World of Sovereignty, is the world of God's eternal Decree (and therefore it is often called the *ʿālam al-lawḥ al-maḥfūẓ*, or the World of the 'Preserved Tablet', where the decree of all beings is preserved), and also the world of the angels. It is the world which is beyond human description and is grasped only by the illumination of intuitive light (*nūr al-baṣīra*) of those whose inner state has attained to the level of the angels and those whose hearts are purified and freed from all the worldly qualities, as a polished mirror reflects the reality, since the heart is of this world of *malakūt*. Ghazālī sometimes calls these two worlds, using the Qur'ānic terms, the *ʿālam al-shahāda* and the *ʿālam al-ghayb* respectively. There is another world between these two, called the *ʿālam al-jabarūt*, or the 'World of Might', which actually means the microcosm of man who is related to the *ʿālam al-malakūt* through his heart and is related to the *ʿālam al-mulk wa'l-shahāda* through his body and senses (*Iḥyā'*, I. 81 [*K. al-ʿIlm*, bāb 6, Āfāt al-ʿilm]; I. 120 [*K. Qawāʿid al-ʿaqā'id*, faṣl 4, Mas'ala fa-in qulta fa-qad . . .]; III. 14 [*K. ʿAjā'ib al-qalb*, Bayān mathal al-qalb]; IV. 244–45 [*K. al-Tawḥīd*, Bayān ḥaqīqat al-tawḥīd]; IV. 288–9 [*K. al-Maḥabba*, Bayān ḥaqīqat al-maḥabba]; and passim; Ghazālī, *Imlā'*, 184–87. See also Wensinck, 'On the Relation between Ghazālī's Cosmology and His Mysticism' and his *La pensée de Ghazzālī*, Ch. III: 'Cosmologie et Mystique'; T. de Boer and L. Gardet, 'ʿĀlam', *EI*², I. 349–52).

to be true'. ᶜUmar heard his speech and said, 'O Emissary of God. How could they hear [you]? How could they answer? They are already stinking'. The Prophet said, 'By Him in Whose Hand lies my soul! You do not hear my word better[114] than they do, it is only that they are unable to reply'. (A tradition in the *Ṣaḥīḥ*.)[115] This is the Prophet's word about the polytheists. As for the believers and martyrs, he said, 'Their spirits are in the crops of green birds,[116] and attached below to the Throne [of God]'. This state [of the spirits] and what is indicated by these words do not exclude [the possibility of] the invocation of God. God has said, *Do not regard as dead those who were slain for the sake of God. Nay, they are alive with God, well supported and rejoicing at the favour that He has brought to them, and are filled with joy for those who remain behind and have not joined them*[117].

Because of the nobility of the remembrance of God[118] (Great and Glorious is He!), the rank of martyrdom [*shahāda*][A] is great. For what is intended [here] is the sealing state [of life] [*khātima*].[B] By the [blessed] sealing state we mean abandonment of the world and coming to God with the heart submerged in Him, with the bonds severed from anything else than Him. If one can make his concern submerged in God (Great and Glorious is He!), he cannot die in that state without being in the line of the fighters [for the sake of God]. For he has severed desire from his blood, his family, his wealth, and his children—to be sure, from all the world. For he wants the world for his life,[119] and his life has now lost its value in his heart for the love of God and the search for His good pleasure. And there is no greater devotion to God than this effort.[120] For this reason, the matter of martyrdom is significant.

[A] In Islam, the martyr (*shahīd*) means one who has died in battle against unbelief.

[B] For more detailed discussion on this subject, see *Iḥyā'*, IV. 170–77 [*K. al-Khawf*, bayān maᶜnā sū' al-khātima (tr. McKane, 64–80)].

Innumerable merits are related about it. One of those is this: when ᶜAbd Allāh ibn ᶜAmr al-Anṣārī was martyred at the Battle of Uḥud,[A] the Emissary of God (may God bless him and grant him peace) said to Jābir (his son),[121] 'Shall I not tell you good news, O Jābir?' He said, 'Yes, may God make you give some good news!' The Emissary of God said, 'God (Great and Glorious is He!) has revived your father and seated him in front of Himself with no veil there between God and him. God said, "Ask Me, O My servant, what you want; I will grant it to you". He said, "O my Lord, You could return me to the world so that I might fight for You and Your Prophet once again". God said, "The divine decree is already issued from Me to the effect that they (the martyrs) shall never return to the world"'.[B] [122]

Death in battle [for the sake of God] is the cause of this [blessed] sealing state. For if one is not killed and remains [alive] for a while, perhaps the desire for the world will come back to him,[123] and it will overcome the remembrance of God (Great and Glorious is He!) which has taken possession of his heart. For this reason, the people of intuitive knowledge [*ahl al-maᶜrifa*] fear a great deal about the [doomed][124] sealing state [of life]. For, even if one's heart adheres to the remembrance of God, it is changeable and is not free from turning back to the lust of the world and is not disconnected from lassitude which soon overcomes it. If a matter of worldly concern[125] appears in his heart at the final state and dominates it, and he passes away from this world in this state, then the domination of the worldly passion over his heart remains and he yearns for the world soon after his death,[126] and desires to return to it. This is because of the paucity of his share in the Afterlife. Indeed, man

[A] This took place in 3 AH.

[B] According to other Traditions, the martyrs are permitted to return to the earth up to ten times for the *jihād* as one of their privileges (W. Björkman, 'Shahīd', *SEI*, 515–17).

dies in the same state as he has lived, and is resurrected in the same state as he has died. So the safest state from this danger is the sealing state of martyrdom, if the intention of the martyr is not to acquire wealth or to be called brave and so forth—as the Tradition[127] says—but love of God and exaltation of His Word.[A]

This is the state which is expressed as follows: *Verily God has bought from the believers their souls and possessions in exchange for Heaven.*[128] A person like this is the one who sells this world for the Afterlife. The state of a martyr corresponds to the meaning of your word: 'There is no god but God'. For he has no aim but God. (He has no object of worship but Him).[129] Each aim is worshipped [*maᶜbūd*], and whatever is worshipped is a deity [*ilāh*]. On the other hand, this martyr is professing, with the tongue of his inner state [*ḥāl*], 'There is no god but God'. For he has no aim but God. He who says this [formula] with his tongue and whose inner state does not support it, his affair is up to the Will of God. No-one is sure about his safety from the danger. For this reason the Emissary of God (may God bless him and grant him peace) preferred the word: 'There is no god but God' to the rest of the invocations.[130] He mentioned this [formula] unconditionally in some places in recommending it. And then, in other places, he mentioned [the conditions of] 'veracity' [*ṣidq*] and 'single-heartedness' [*ikhlāṣ*].[131] He once said, 'He who says, "There is no god but God" single-heartedly . . . .' The meaning of

[A] It is related that the Prophet said: 'A man has been doing good deeds of the People of Heaven for seventy years so that they suppose that he is a member of their group and there is left only a span of the hand between him and Heaven. Then his fortune turns against him and he commits an evil deed of the People of Hell, and goes directly to Hell'. Man really does not know his 'sealing state of life' until its end actually comes. This fear always makes the Sufis cautious against conceit (*ᶜujb*), even at their higher stage (*Iḥyā'*, IV. 45 [*Tawba*, rukn 3, bayān aqsām al-ᶜibād]).

'single-heartedness'[A] is that the inner state [*ḥāl*] renders support to the pronouncement [*maqāl*].

We ask God (Exalted is He!) to make us, at the sealing state, one of the people of the formula: 'There is no god but God' in state and in pronouncement, both outwardly and inwardly, so that we may bid farewell to the world, without turning back to it any more, disgusted at it, with love of meeting God. 'He who desires to meet God, He desires to meet him. He who hates to meet God, He hates to meet him.'[132] These are some allusions to the meaning of invocation, to which one cannot add more in the science of religious practices.

[A] This is one of the key concepts in Ghazālī's thought. Originally it meant 'to keep something clear and pure, or free from mixture'. In the Qur'ān, it is mostly used to mean 'absolute devotion to God' in opposition to *ishrāk* (L. Gardet, 'Ikhlāṣ', *EI*², III. 1059–60). Furthermore, according to Ghazālī, it means that man's action is motivated by a single pure intention. For example, when a man gives alms, his motive is not mixed with vanity, fame, and so forth. And finally it means to orient man's every single thought and act for the supreme goal of the Meeting with God in the next world. This is called the 'absolute single-heartedness' [*ikhlāṣ muṭlaq*]. (For more details, see *Iḥyā'*, IV. [*K. al-Nīya*].)

CHAPTER TWO

On the Forms and Value of Supplication and Some Transmitted Prayers; the Merit of Asking For Forgiveness and of Invoking Blessing Upon the Emissary of God

The Merit of Supplication

GOD (Exalted is He!) has said, *If my servants ask you about Me,* [*say:*] *I am near, and I respond to the supplication of a suppliant when he makes it to Me. Therefore let them call for My response.*[1] God has also said, *Supplicate unto your Lord humbly and secretly. Verily, He loves not the transgressors.*[2] He has also said, *Your Lord has said, 'Supplicate unto Me, and I will answer you. Verily those who refuse the act of My worship out of haughtiness will enter Hell in a wretched state'.*[3] He has said, *Say, 'Supplicate unto God, or supplicate unto the Merciful; whichsoever you may call, His are the most beautiful Names'.*[4]

Al-Nuᶜmān ibn Bas͟hīr related that the Prophet (may God bless him and grant him peace) said, 'Verily supplication is the [real] worship' and that he recited [from the Qur'ān], *Supplicate unto Me, and I will answer you.*[5]

The Emissary of God (may God bless him and grant him

peace) said, 'Supplication is the marrow of worship'.[A] [6]

Abū Hurayra related that the Emissary of God (may God bless him and grant him peace) said, 'Nothing is dearer to God than supplication'.[B] [7]

The Emissary of God (may God bless him and grant him peace) said, 'One of three things never fails to come to a man from supplication: either a sin is forgiven him, or something good comes hurriedly to him, or something good is stored up for him'.[8]

Abū Dharr (may God be pleased with him) said, 'One needs for piety as much supplication as one needs salt for food'.

The Emissary of God (may God bless him and grant him peace) said, 'Ask God for His favour. Verily God likes to be asked. The most meritorious act of worship is expectation [*intiẓār*] of relief [from distress]'.[9]

PROPRIETIES OF SUPPLICATION, WHICH ARE TEN IN NUMBER

1. *The noble time is to be chosen for supplication, such as the day of ʿArafa*[C] *from the year, Ramaḍān*[D] *from the months, Friday*[E] *from the week, and the moment of daybreak from the night-time:*

God (Exalted is He!) has said, *At daybreak they used to ask for*

[A] For, according to Zabīdī, the suppliant supplicates unto God only when he gives up the hope of resorting to anything else but God. This is the essence of *tawḥīd* and *ikhlāṣ*, above which there is no worship. It is the expression of the human lack of—and need of—power and might. And this is the sign of creatureliness (*ʿubūdīya*) and the acknowledgement of the meanness of humanity (*basharīya*) (Zabīdī, v. 29).

[B] For supplication expresses the power of God and the impotence of the suppliant (Zabīdī, v. 29).

[C] See note A on p. 5 above.

[D] This is the ninth lunar month, during which the annual fast is observed.

[E] The Muslim holy day, when the public worship is carried out.

forgiveness.[10] The Emissary of God (may God bless him and grant him peace) said, 'Every night God descends to the lowest heaven, when one-third of the night remains. He says, "I will answer him who supplicates to Me. I will grant unto him who beseeches Me. I will forgive him who asks Me for forgiveness" '.[11]

It is related that Jacob (upon whom be peace) said (to his sons)[12] the word: *'I shall* [sawfa] *beseech my Lord for forgiveness for you'*[13] meaning only to supplicate [unto God] at daybreak, and it is said that he rose at daybreak in order to supplicate while his sons were behind him, saying Amen, and then God (Great and Glorious is He!) revealed to him, 'I have forgiven them and made them prophets'.

2. *The noble state is to be taken as an opportunity for supplication:*

Abū Hurayra (may God be pleased with him) said, 'The doors of Heaven are opened when lines [of fighters] march for the sake of God, and when rain pours down in torrents, and at the time of the *iqāma*[A] of the prescribed ritual prayers. So take these opportunities for supplication'.[14]

Mujāhid said, 'Verily the ritual prayer was laid on the best hours, so you should make supplication after the ritual prayers'.

The Emissary of God (may God bless him and grant him peace) said, 'Supplication [made] between the *adhān*[B] and the *iqāma* is never rejected'.[15]

He also said (may God bless him and grant him peace), 'The supplication of a fasting man is never rejected'.[16]

[A] The *adhān* is the call to prayer; the announcement of the arrival of the ritual prayer time, made from the minaret. The *iqāma* is the announcement, made in the mosque, that the prayer is ready to begin. The wording of the *iqāma* is slightly different from that of the *adhān*. (See Lane, *Lexicon*, 43.)
[B] See above.

Truly the nobility of the hours relies upon the nobility of the states. Thus the moment of daybreak is the time when the heart is pure, sincere, and free from disturbances.[17] The day of ᶜArafa and Friday are the times when the aspirations [of the Muslims] are united and the hearts co-operate with each other asking for the abundant flow of God's mercy. This is one of the reasons for the nobility of the hours, not to mention the mystery hidden in them which man cannot know.

The posture of prostration [*sujūd*] must also be especially appropriate to receive the divine response. Abū Hurayra (may God be pleased with him) related that the Prophet (may God bless him and grant him peace) said, 'Man is nearest to God when he prostrates. So make many supplications at that time'.[18]

Ibn ᶜAbbās (may God be pleased with him) related that the Prophet (may God bless him and grant him peace) said, 'Verily I refrained from reciting the Qur'ān while bowing and prostrating. While you are bowing, glorify the Lord. While you are prostrating, make supplication earnestly, for it is a suitable time for your request to be heard'.[19]

3. *Supplication is to be made in the direction of the* qibla, *with the hands so high that the whiteness of the armpits can be seen:*

Jābir ibn ᶜAbd Allāh said, 'The Emissary of God (may God bless him and grant him peace) came to the halting place [*mawqif*] on the day of ᶜArafa[A] and turned toward the *qibla* and kept supplicating till the sun set'.[20]

Salmān related that the Emissary of God (may God bless him and grant him peace) said, 'Verily your Lord is living and generous; He feels too ashamed, when His servants raise their hands toward Him, to return them empty'.[21]

Anas related, 'The Emissary of God (may God bless him and

[A] See note A on p.5 above.

grant him peace) used to raise his hands so high that the white parts of his armpits were seen during supplication, but not pointing with his two fingers'.[22]

Abū Hurayra (may God be pleased with him) related that the Emissary of God (may God bless him and grant him peace), passing by a man who was making supplication, pointing his two forefingers [*iṣbaᶜ sabbāba*], said, 'Make it one, make it one'[23]—meaning 'Be restricted to one finger'.

Abu'l-Dardā' (may God be pleased with him) said, 'Raise these hands [for supplication] before iron handcuffs are put on them'.

Then one must wipe one's face with the hands at the end of supplication. ᶜUmar (may God be pleased with him) said, 'When the Emissary of God stretched his hands in supplication, he never withdrew them until he wiped his face with them'.[24]

Ibn ᶜAbbās said, 'When the Emissary of God (may God bless him and grant him peace) made supplication, he joined together his hands and held their palms toward his face'.[25]

These are the positions of the hands, and one should not look up toward heaven. The Emissary of God (may God bless him and grant him peace) said, 'Let the people stop raising their eyes up toward heaven during supplication, otherwise their eyes will be dazzled'.[A] [26]

4. *The voice is to be modulated between silent and loud:*

This is due to the Tradition related by Abū Mūsā al-A<u>sh</u>ᶜarī: 'We were marching with the Emissary of God (may God bless him and grant him peace). When we came close to Medina, he said, "God is most great!" So the people said, "God is most great!" and raised their voices. Thereupon the Prophet said,

[A] As Zabīdī shows. there are contradictory Traditions which approve the raising of the eyes up at the sky as the *qibla* of supplication (Zabīdī, v. 35–6. See also below, 44, 54, and 87, and <u>Gh</u>azālī, *al-Ḥikma fī ma<u>kh</u>lūqāt Allāh*, 18.)

"O people! Verily He Whom you are calling upon is not deaf nor absent. He Whom you are calling upon is just between you and the necks of your camels" '.[27]

ᶜĀ'isha (may God be pleased with her), commenting on the word of God, *Be not loud in your worship* [ṣalāt], *nor yet silent therein*[28] said, 'Namely, during your supplication [*duᶜā'*]'.[A]

God praised His prophet Zacharia (upon whom be peace), *when he called upon his Lord secretly.*[29]

God has said, *Supplicate unto your Lord humbly and secretly.*[30]

5. *Supplication is not to be weighed with the* sajᶜ *style:*[B]

The attitude of the suppliant must be that of a humble person, and presumptuous effort [*takalluf*] does not befit him. The Emissary of God (may God bless him and grant him peace) said, 'People will go beyond the bounds in prayer'.[31] And God has said, *Supplicate unto your Lord humbly and secretly. Verily He loves not the transgressors*:[32] it is said that the reference in this instance is to a presumptuous effort in the *sajᶜ*-style. The best thing is not to go beyond [the limits of] the transmitted prayers. For man is sometimes extravagant and asks for what his proper interest does not require.

[A] Or during your recitation (*qirā'a*) of the Qur'ān in the ritual prayer, as is understood by most exegetes (Ṭabarī, XV. 113; Zamakhsharī, II. 470; *Jalālayn*, 266).

[B] A rhymed prose, a mode of rhetoric which has words occurring at short intervals in rhyme but not bound by metre. Probably this was the earliest mode of elevated expression practiced by the Arabs before the development of the regular metres, and it was the style used by the Kāhins and poets (*shāᶜir*). Ghazālī says that the *sajᶜ* style is 'a presumptuous effort in speech' (below, and p.38), and this is true if we take into consideration the re-introduction and cultivation of this style by the secretarial class represented by Ibn Nubāta (d. 374/984–5). However, the original reason for the suppression of its usage in prayer is said to be its association with the Arab paganism represented by the Kāhins and poets (Krenkow, art. 'Sajᶜ', in *EI*[1], IV. 43–4; Goldziher, 'Zauberelemente', 303; idem, 'Über die Vorgeschichte der Hiğā'-Poesie', 57–76).

Not everybody is good at making supplication. For this reason, it is related from Muᶜādh (may God be pleased with him): 'Learned men are needed in Paradise. For it is said to the people of Paradise: "Wish!" but they do not know how to do it until they learn [it] from the learned men'.

The Emissary of God (may God bless him and grant him peace) said, 'Beware of the *sajᶜ*-style in supplication! It suffices for any of you to say, "O God! I ask You for Heaven, and the word and work which bring us thereto. I take refuge with You from Hell, and the word and work which bring us thereto" '.[33]

A Tradition says, 'There will come people who go beyond the proper bounds in supplication and ritual purification'.

One of the Ancients [*salaf*] passed by a popular preacher [*qāṣṣ*] who was making supplication in the *sajᶜ*-style. He said to this man, 'Are you trying to exaggerate to God? I swear that I saw Ḥabīb al-ᶜAjamī supplicating, and his words did not go beyond this: "O God, make us upright.[34] O God, put us not to shame on the Day of Judgement. O God, help us to do good". The people from every province were supplicating behind him, and he knew the blessing of his supplication'.

Someone said, 'Supplicate with the tongue of submissiveness and humbleness, not the tongue of eloquence and unrestraint'.

It is said that learned men and substitute-saints [*abdāl*][A] did not exceed seven words or less in supplication. The end of the Sūra of the Cow[35] testifies to this point, for God never taught His servants on any occasion prayers longer than that.

[A] Pl. of *badal* ('substitute'). According to the Sufi doctrine, the cosmic order is maintained by a certain number of saints, so that when a holy person dies his place is immediately filled by a 'substitute'. There is no unanimity about the number of the *abdāl* and their position in the saintly hierarchy headed by the *quṭb*, or 'pole' (Nicholson, art. 'Badal', *SEI*, 55; Hujwīrī, 213–4; *Iḥyā'*, III. 347–8 [*K. Dhamm al-kibr*, Bayān al-akhlāq]; see also Goldziher, 'Arabische Synonymik der Askese', *Der Islam* 8 [1918], 210–3).

Know that the aim of *saj*ᶜ is a presumptuous effort in speech, and this is not appropriate to humbleness and submissiveness. It is true that there are rhymed speeches transmitted from the Emissary of God, but they are not pretentious. For example, he said: 'I ask You for security on the Day of the Threat [*yawm al-wa*ᶜ*īd*] and for Paradise on the Day of Eternity [*yawm al-khulūd*], together with those who are brought near [to God][A] and witnessing [*shuhūd*][B], those who often bow and prostrate [*sujūd*],[C] and keep their covenants [ᶜ*uhūd*][D]. Verily You are compassionate and affectionate [*wadūd*], and You do what You will [*turīd*]'[36]—and the like.[E] So let a man confine himself to transmitted prayers, or let him beg with the tongue of humbleness and submissiveness without using the *saj*ᶜ-style and constraint, for it is humbleness that God loves.

6. *Humbleness, submissiveness, longing* [raghba], *and fear* [rahba]:

God (Exalted is He!) has said, *They were competing with one*

[A] In the Qur'ān, *al-muqarrabūn* is used in reference to a class of angels who praise God, day and night without ceasing, around the Throne (Q. IV:172; XXI:20) and also to human beings, specifically Jesus (III:45) because of his semi-angelic character (Wensinck, art. 'Malā'ika', *SEI*, 318–20). Ghazālī generally stresses its association with humans, i.e. those who have attained the angelic character or the highest state of the Sufi, although he does not neglect the cosmological aspect (*Iḥyā'*, IV. 187 [*K. al-Faqr*, Bayān ḥaqīqat al-faqr muṭlaq[an]]; IV. 210 [*K. al-Faqr*, Bayān aḥwāl al-sā'ilīn]; IV. 351 [*K. al-Maḥabba*, Khātima]; and passim).

[B] A reference to the Beatific Vision.

[C] Cf. Q. XLVIII:29; XCVI:19. Ghazālī quotes a Tradition to the effect that ᶜAlī ibn ᶜAbd Allāh ibn ᶜAbbās was nicknamed 'the Prostrator' (*al-sajjād*) because he used to perform a thousand prostrations every day (*Iḥyā'*, I. 149 [*K. al-Ṣalāt*, bāb 1, Faḍā'il al-sujūd]).

[D] For the meaning of ᶜ*uhūd* (pl. of ᶜ*ahd*), see below p.54 n.A and Zabīdī, V. 64.

[E] See Zabīdī, V. 38 for some other examples.

another in [doing] good deeds and supplicating unto Us in longing and in fear.[37]

He has said (Great and Glorious is He!), *Supplicate unto your Lord humbly and secretly.*[38]

The Emissary of God (may God bless him and grant him peace) said, 'When God loves a man, He puts him on trial until He hears his humble request'.[39]

7. *Supplication is to be direct and unconditional; the response is to be firmly believed in, and hope in it is to be sincere.*[A]

The Emissary of God (may God bless him and grant him peace) said, 'Let not any of you say in supplication, "O God, forgive me if You will! Have mercy on me if You will!"—he should instead ask directly, since there is no one who compels [*mukrih*] Him'.[40]

He said (may God bless him and grant him peace), 'When any of you supplicates, let him make big requests. For nothing competes with God in greatness'.[41]

He said (may God bless him and grant him peace), 'Supplicate to God with firm conviction of His response. Know that God (Great and Glorious is He!) never answers the supplication of him whose heart is heedless'.[42]

Sufyān ibn ʿUyayna said, 'Let not any of you give up supplication because of what he knows about himself. For God answered even the supplication of the worst creature, Iblīs,[B] when he said, *"My Lord, give me respite until the day when they are resurrected!" and He said, "You are among those who are given respite"*[43]'.

[A] That is, to have a firm faith in the good intention (*ḥusn al-ẓann*) of God, even though the response does not come as expected, and to have the expectation of response predominant in the heart over that of rejection. This is the sincerity of hope (*ṣidq al-rajā'*) (Zabīdī, v. 39).

[B] That is, Satan.

8. *Supplication is to be made earnestly*[A] *and repeated three times:*

Ibn Masᶜūd said that when the Emissary of God (upon whom be peace) supplicated, he supplicated three times, and that when he asked, he asked three times.[44] One should not wait impatiently for the response, according to the word of the Emissary of God (may God bless him and grant him peace): 'Any of you will be answered so long as he is not so anxious as to complain, [saying], "I have prayed, but I have not been answered yet".[B] So when you supplicate, ask God much. For you are supplicating to a Generous One'.[45]

Someone said, 'I have been asking God (Great and Glorious is He!) for a certain thing for twenty years. But He has not responded to me, while I keep hoping for the response. I asked God to help me leave behind what does not concern me'.

The Emissary of God (may God bless him and grant him peace) said, 'When any of you asks God for something, and he has known the answer, then he should say, "Praise be to God, by Whose grace good deeds are fulfilled!" And he whose supplication is late in being heard, let him say, "Praise be to God, under all conditions [*ᶜalā kull ḥāl*]!" '[C] [46]

[A] *al-ilḥāḥ fī al-duᶜā'*: originally the form of supplication in which holy names, persons, and things are repeated in order to petition God, as is seen in Abū Bakr's prayer (below, p.60–1). (Goldziher, 'Zauberelemente', 318.

[B] That is, not to be impatient and irritated about the delay of the answer, as though one had the right to do so. In fact, no one has any rights over God. There may be profit in delay; furthermore, supplication is worship and submission, and impatience and irritation are in contradiction to them. (Zabīdī, v. 39.)

[C] For all the conditions of a Muslim, says Zabīdī, are good, and God's decree of 'joy' and 'distress' for him is mercy and grace. If the veil were removed, he would be more pleased with 'distress' than with 'joy'. God knows what profits His servants better than they. (Zabīdī, v. 40.)

9. *Supplication is to be begun with the invocation of God, not with petition:*

Salama ibn al-Akwaᶜ said, 'I have never heard the Emissary of God (may God bless him and grant him peace) beginning supplication without this invocation: "Glory be to my Lord, the Supreme, the Most Exalted, the Generous Giver!" '[47]

Abū Sulaymān al-Dārānī (may God show him His mercy) said, 'Let him who wishes to ask God for a need begin with the blessing upon the Prophet (may God bless him and grant him peace) and then let him ask God for his need, and end with the blessing upon the Prophet. For God surely accepts the two blessings, and He is too generous to leave unanswered the request submitted between these two blessings'.

It is related in a Tradition that the Emissary of God (may God bless him and grant him peace) said, 'When you ask God for something, begin with the blessing upon me. For God is too generous for it to happen that, being given two requests, He meets one of them, leaving the other unanswered'.[48] This is related by Abū Ṭālib al-Makkī.

10. *The inward attitude, which is the root for the response—repentance, rejection of evil deeds, and turning toward God with the utmost effort. This is the direct cause of the response:*

Kaᶜb al-Aḥbār related, 'A severe drought befell the people in the time of Moses, the Emissary of God. He went out with the children of Israel and prayed with them for rain. However, they did not have rain. So he went out three times, but they did not have rain. Then God (Great and Glorious is He!) revealed to Moses (upon whom be peace), "Verily I will not respond to you, for there is a slanderer among you". Moses asked, "O my Lord, who is he? [Tell us] so that we can expel him from among us". And God revealed to Moses, "O Moses, I am prohibiting you from slandering, and can I become

Myself a slanderer?" Moses said to the children of Israel, "Repent of slander to your Lord, all of you". And they repented and then He sent rain upon them'.[A]

Saʿīd ibn Jubayr said, 'At the time of a king of the children of Israel, the people suffered from a drought. So they prayed for rain. Then the king said to the children of Israel, "Let God send rain [*samā'*] to us, or let us torment Him". On being asked, "How can you torment Him while He is high up in heaven?" he said, "I will kill His friends [*awliyā'*] and the men who are obedient to Him. This will be a torment for Him". So God sent down rain upon them'.[B]

Sufyān al-Thawrī said, 'I was told: "The children of Israel were so afflicted with drought for seven years that finally they ate corpses among dunghills and devoured infants. Under these circumstances, they went out into the mountains, weeping and imploring. Thereupon God revealed to their prophet, 'Even if you walked to Me on your feet until your knees were sore and your hands reached the clouds in the sky and your tongues became tired with prayer, I would not respond to you, O suppliants, and would not have mercy upon you, O weepers, until you right the wrongs which you have done to people'. And they did so, and had rain that same day" '.

Mālik ibn Dīnār said, 'Drought befell the people among the children of Israel, and they went out several times [to pray for rain]. Then God (Great and Glorious is He!) revealed to their prophet, "Let them know: 'You come out unto Me with impure bodies, and you raise your hands with which you shed blood, and you fill your stomachs with unlawful food. So now

[A] For the prayer for rain, see A. Bel, art. 'Istisqā'' in *SEI*, 187–88, to whose bibliography should be added Goldziher, 'Zauberelemente'; Mittwoch, 'Zur Entstehungsgeschichte'; E. Westermarck, *Ritual and Belief in Morocco*, II. 254–58, and the references quoted therein.

[B] This is one of the typical examples of the adjurative oath [*munāshada*]. The underlying idea is that one can influence God by threatening Him (Goldziher, 'Zauberelemente', 304–11).

My anger with you has increased, and you will become even more distant in estrangement from Me' " '.

Abu'l-Ṣadīq al-Nājī said, 'Solomon (upon whom be peace) once went out to pray for rain and passed by an ant which was thrown on its back and raising its legs up toward heaven. It was saying, "O God, verily we are one [kind] of Your creatures, and we cannot dispense with Your sustenance. So do not destroy us on account of the sins of others!" Thereupon Solomon said [to his people], "Go back. You have already been given water by virtue of another's supplication" '.

Al-Awzā^{c}ī said, 'The people went out to pray for rain. Bilāl ibn Sa^{c}d stood before them, and praised and eulogised God. Then he said, "O people, who are present here! Are you not confessing your evil deeds?" They said, "O God, yes!" He said, "O God, surely we heard You saying, *There is no way [of blame] against those who do good.*[49] And we have already confessed our evil deeds. Is Your forgiveness not for the likes of us? O God, forgive us! Have mercy upon us! Give us rain!" He raised his hands, and his people raised their hands: and they were given rain'.

On being requested, 'Supplicate unto God for us', Mālik ibn Dīnār said, "Verily you are waiting impatiently for rain, and I am waiting impatiently for stones" '.

It is related: 'Jesus (upon whom be peace) once went out to pray for rain. When the people were displeased[50] [with the outcome], he said to them, "Let any of you who has committed sins go back". At this, all of them returned, and nobody remained with him in the desert except one. So Jesus said to him, "Have you no sin?" He said, "By God! I do not know anything about it except this. One day I was performing ritual prayer, when a woman passed by me. I glanced at her with my eye. So when she passed away, I thrust my finger into my eye and plucked it out. And I followed her with that eye".[A] Jesus

[A] Cf. Matthew, 18:19.

said to him, "Supplicate unto God until I say Amen to your supplication". So the man supplicated. Then the clouds spread in the sky and bent down, and they were granted rain" '.

Yaḥyā al-Ghassānī said, 'The people were afflicted with drought at the time of David. So they chose three out of their learned men, and went out to pray for rain with them. One of the learned men said, "O God, verily You have revealed in Your Torah that we should forgive him who has wronged us. O God, verily we have wronged ourselves! So forgive us!" The second said, "O God, verily You have revealed in Your Torah that we should set free our slaves. O God, verily we are Your slaves. Set us free!" The third said, "O God, verily You have revealed in Your Torah that we should not refuse the wretched when they stand at our doors. O God, verily we are Your wretched people, who stand at Your door. Do not refuse our supplication!" Then rain came to them'.

ᶜAṭā' al-Salīmī said, 'We were deprived of rain. So we went out to pray for rain and came across Saᶜdūn al-Majnūn in the graveyard. He looked at me and said, "O ᶜAṭā', is this the Day of Resurrection or the day when *what is in the graves is raised and brought forth*[51]?" I said, "No, [this is because] we have not been given rain. So we came out to pray for it". He said, "O ᶜAṭā', [did you come] with earthly hearts or heavenly ones?" I said, "With heavenly hearts". He said, "Far from it! O ᶜAṭā', say to those who adorn themselves: 'Do not adorn yourselves! For the Examiner has a penetrating insight' ". Then he glanced up at heaven and said, "My God, my Master, my Lord! Do not destroy Your country because of the sins of Your servants! But by the hidden secret of Your names and those of Your favours which the veils conceal, [I implore You] that You grant us plentiful and sweet water, by which You give life to man and by which You water the country. O You Who are powerful over everything!" No sooner had he finished his speech than the sky trembled and was filled with lightning, and rain came as though from the mouth of a waterskin. Then he went away, reciting:

Happy are the ascetics[A] and the ardent worshippers,[B]
for they have emptied their stomachs for the sake of
their Lord.
They keep their ailing eyes awake out of love
and their night is spent while they are vigilant.
They are so occupied with worshipping God
that the people have thought them demented'.

Ibn al-Mubārak said, 'I went up to Medina in the year of severe drought. The people went out to pray for rain, so I went out with them. There appeared a black youth in two pieces of sackcloth. He wrapped his body with one of them and covered his shoulders with the other. He sat beside me and I heard him saying, "O My Lord, numerous sins and evil deeds have dulled our faces in Your sight. You have withdrawn rain from us so that You may thereby discipline Your servants. I beseech You, O Affectionate One, Possessor of Patience, O You of Whom Your servants know only benificence, to give them rain right now!" Scarcely had he finished the words "right now", when the sky became cloudy and rain poured down on every side. Then I went to al-Fuḍayl and he said [to me], "What is the matter? You look sad". So I said, "There was an affair in which somebody came before us and he, rather than we, carried it out", and I told the story to him. Then al-Fuḍayl screamed and fell down in a faint'.

[A] The ascetics (*zāhidūn*—or *zuhhād*, pl. of *zāhid*) refer to those who shun not only the legally prohibited things (the virtue of *waraᶜ*), but worldly things in general, or the world itself (for the sake of the Afterlife). For a full discussion about this, see *Iḥyā'*, IV. 211–37 [*K. al-Faqr*, s̲h̲aṭr 2], and also M. Smith, *An Early Mystic*, 169.

[B] The 'ardent worshippers' (*ᶜābidūn*—or *ᶜubbād*, pl. of *ᶜābid*) are 'those who devote themselves to the pious service of God' (Goldziher, *Le Dogme*, 121).

It is related that ᶜUmar ibn al-Khaṭṭāb once prayed for rain with al-ᶜAbbās. When ᶜUmar finished his prayer, al-ᶜAbbās said, 'O God, no trial has come down from heaven except for sin, and it is not removed except by repentance. So the people have brought me to You because of my special relationship to Your Prophet. These are our hands raised to You with our sins and these are our foreheads with repentance. You are the Shepherd and do not neglect a single stray sheep, and do not set the wretched in a doomed abode. The small are already humble. The great are ashamed. The voices are raised with complaint. *You know the secret and that which is yet more hidden.*[52] O God, relieve them with Your help before they despair and perish. *For no one despairs of the mercy of God save the disbelieving people*[53]'. No sooner had he finished his speech than the sky was raised up like a mountain.

THE MERIT OF INVOKING BLESSING UPON THE EMISSARY OF GOD,[A] AND HIS VIRTUE

God (Exalted is He!) has said, *Verily God and His angels send blessing upon the Prophet. O you who believe! Invoke blessing upon him and ask for peace upon him!*[54]

It is related: 'One day the Emissary of God (may God bless him and grant him peace) came, good tidings being visible on his face, and said, "Gabriel (upon whom be peace) came to me and asked, 'Are you not happy, O Muḥammad, that no-one of your Community ever invokes blessing upon you without my invoking blessing upon him ten times, and no one of your Community ever asks for peace upon you without my asking for peace upon him?' " '[55]

The Emissary of God (may God bless him and grant him

[A] As to the etymology and meaning of *taṣliya*, the development of its formula in the historical context, and its usage, see E. Calverley, *Worship in Islam*, 3–6; Goldziher, 'Über dir Eulogien des Muhammedaner', 97–128; C. Padwick, *Muslim Devotions*, 152–6.

peace) said, 'The angels invoke blessing upon him who invokes blessing upon me, for as long as he invokes blessing upon me. So let him increase or decrease [blessing] by the angels [upon himself as he pleases]'.[56]

He said, 'The closest of people to me is he who invokes blessing [upon me] most'.[57]

He said, 'For the believer, it is enough stinginess [*bukhl*] not to invoke blessing upon me when my name is mentioned in his presence'.[58]

He said, 'Invoke blessing frequently upon me on Friday'.[59]

He said, 'For any one of my Community who invokes blessing upon me are written ten good deeds and erased ten evil deeds'.[60]

He said, 'My Intercession shall become lawful for whoeover, on hearing the *adhān* and the *iqāma*, says, "O God, Lord of this completed call and initiated ritual prayer. Send blessing upon Muḥammad, Your servant and Your Emissary. Give him mediation, virtue, the exalted rank, and intercession on the Day of Resurrection" '.[61]

He said, 'Whoever invokes blessing upon me in writing, the angels never cease asking for forgiveness for his sake as long as my name is in that book'.[62]

He said, 'Verily there are angels hovering over the earth who carry to me the greeting for peace from my Community'.[63]

He said, 'No one asks for peace upon me but that God returns my spirit to me so that I may return the prayer to him'.[64]

On being asked, 'O Emissary of God, how shall we invoke blessing upon you?' he said, 'Say: "O God, send blessing upon Muḥammad, Your servant, and upon his family and his wives and his descendants, as You did send blessing upon Abraham and his family. Send grace upon Muḥammad, his wives and his descendants as You did send grace upon Abraham and his family. Verily You are praiseworthy and glorious" '.[65]

It is related that ʿUmar ibn al-Khaṭṭāb (may God be pleased with him), after the death of the Emissary of God (may God bless him and grant him peace), was heard weeping and saying, 'You are dearer to me than my father and my mother, O Emissary of God! Once there was a palm-trunk beside which you spoke to the people. When the number of the people increased, you took a pulpit [*minbar*][A] so that you might make yourself heard. Then the palm-trunk moaned because of your departure, so you put your hand on it and it became silent. Now your Community is more entitled to grieve for you as you have departed from them. You are dearer to me than my father and my mother, O Emissary of God! Your virtue has reached such a degree that He has equated obedience to you with obedience to Himself. For He has said, *He who obeys the Emissary has obeyed God.*[66] You are dearer to me than my father and my mother, O Messenger of God! Your virtue has reached such a degree that God informed you that He had forgiven you before He let you know your sin. For He has said, *God has forgiven you.* [*But*] *why did you give them leave?*[B] [67] You are dearer to me than my father and my mother, O Emissary of God! Your merit has reached such a degree that He sent you as the last of the prophets but mentioned you in the first of them. For He has said, *Therefore We took a covenant from the prophets—from you, from Noah, from Abraham.*[68] You are dearer to me than my father and my mother, O Emissary of God! Your virtue has reached such a degree that the people of Hell wish that they had obeyed you, while they are being punished between the layers of Hell, saying, *Would that we had obeyed God and the Emissary of God!*[69] You are dearer to me than my father and mother, O Emissary of God! Verily God gave Moses, son of ʿImrān, a rock from which the streams of water

[A] For the origin of this, see Pedersen, art. 'Masdjid' (under 'Minbar'), in *SEI*, 343–5.

[B] God is speaking to the Prophet about those who came to him asking for leave so that they might escape from the *jihād* (Cf. Q. IX:44–8).

welled up. But this is not so miraculous as your fingers, when water gushed forth from them.[70] You are dearer to me than my father and my mother, O Emissary of God! Verily God gave Solomon, son of David, *the wind, whose morning course was a month's journey and the evening course a month's journey*.[71] But this is not so miraculous as the Burāq[A] on which you ascended up to the seventh heaven and then you offered the morning prayer, after waking up from your night on the valley floor [*al-abṭaḥ*].[B] May God bless you! You are dearer to me than my father and my mother, O Emissary of God! Verily God let Jesus, son of Mary, revive the dead. But this was not so miraculous as the poisoned sheep, which, though roasted, spoke to you. Its leg said to you, "Eat me not, for I am poisoned!"[72] You are dearer to me than my father and my mother, O Emissary of God! Once Noah cursed his people, and said, *"My Lord, leave not upon the earth any one of the unbelievers"*.[73] If you cursed us in the same way, we should all perish. Your back was trampled and your face was made to bleed, and your teeth near the incisor were broken. But you refrained from saying anything but good.[C] And you said, "O God, forgive my people, for verily they do not know". You are dearer to me than my father and my mother, O Emissary of God! In spite of your young age and your short life, you were obeyed by many more than obeyed Noah in spite of his old age and his long life. Many people believe in you, but he had only a few who believed in him. You are dearer to me than my father and my mother, O Emissary of God! If you had not sat together with any but an equal to you, you would not

[A] This was a miraculous riding animal between the sizes of a mule and an ass, having two wings. It was so called because of the intense whiteness of its hue and its great brightness, or because of the swiftness of its motion, like lightning (Zabīdī, v. 53; Hughes, 44; Lane, *Lexicon*, 191).

[B] This is the place known as al-Maḥṣab (Zabīdī, v. 53), or the Wādī of Mecca (Wāqidī, II. 809, n.2).

[C] At the Battle of Uḥud, which took place in 3 AH.

have sat together with us. If you had not married any but an equal to you, you would not have married among us. If you had not trusted any but an equal to you, you would not have trusted us. But surely you did sit together with us; you did marry among us; you did trust us; you did wear wool; you did ride on a donkey and I rode behind you; you did put your food on the ground; you did lick your fingers out of your humbleness. May God send blessing and peace upon you!'

Someone said, 'I used to write Traditions and invoke blessing upon the Prophet but without asking for peace upon him. Then I saw the Prophet in a dream, and he said to me, "Do you not complete the greeting to me [in your writing]?" Since then I never fail to invoke blessing and peace upon him, when I write'.

It was related that Abu'l-Ḥasan [al-S̲h̲āfiᶜī] said, 'I saw the Prophet (may God bless him and grant him peace) in a dream, and I said, "O Emissary of God! With what was al-S̲h̲āfiᶜī rewarded on your behalf when he invoked in his book, the *Risāla*:[A] 'May God send blessing upon Muḥammad!—a phrase which the mindful invoke and the heedless forget to invoke?' " Then he said (may God bless him and grant him peace), "He was rewarded on my behalf that he might not have to stand for the reckoning of his sins" '.

THE MERIT OF ASKING FOR FORGIVENESS

God (Great and Glorious is He!) has said, *Those who, when they have committed a vile deed or wronged themselves, remember God and ask for forgiveness of their sins. . .*[74]

ᶜAlqama and al-Aswad related that ᶜAbd Allāh ibn Masᶜūd (may God be pleased with him) said, 'In the Book of God there

[A] This is the famous *Risāla*, whose full title is *Kitāb al-Risāla fī uṣūl al-fiqh*, i.e. S̲h̲āfiᶜī's epistle supposedly addressed to ᶜAbd al-Raḥmān ibn Mahdī (d. 198/813–4) (Zabīdī, v. 55; M. Khadduri [trans.], *Islamic Jurisprudence: S̲h̲āfiᶜī's* Risāla).

are two [special] verses. Whenever a servant commits a sin and recites these two verses and asks God for forgiveness, He will forgive him. [They are] His Word: *Those who, when they have committed a vile deed or wronged themselves, remember God and ask for forgiveness of their sins. . .* and His Word: *He who, doing evil or wronging himself, asks for forgiveness, will find Him All-Forgiving and Merciful*'.[75]

God has said, *Then sing the praise of your Lord and ask Him for forgiveness. Verily He is the Oft-Relenting.*[76]

He has said, *Those who ask for forgiveness at the break of dawn. . .*[77]

The Emissary of God (may God bless him and grant him peace) used frequently to say, 'Glory be to You! O God, praise be to You! O God, forgive me! Verily You are the Merciful Forgiver'.[78]

He said (may God bless him and grant him peace), 'To him who often asks God for forgiveness, He gives release from every fear, a way out from every distress, and gives sustenance from where he does not expect'.[79]

He said (may God bless him and grant him peace), 'Verily I ask God for forgiveness and turn back to Him repenting seventy times a day'.[80] This was so in spite of the fact he was forgiven his *former and forthcoming* sins.[81]

He said (may God bless him and grant him peace), 'Verily my heart becomes covered so that I ask God for forgiveness a hundred times a day'.[82]

He said (may God bless him and grant him peace), 'Whoever, when he goes to bed, says three times, "I ask God for forgiveness, the great God, beside Whom there is no god, the Living, the Self-Subsisting, and I repent to Him", God will forgive his sins even if they are like the foam of the sea, or the sand of [c]Ālij,[A] or the leaves of the trees, or the days of the

[A] A place in the domain of the Tamīm tribe in North Arabia (Zabīdī, v. 57). For all these and other similar hyperbolic expressions, see Goldziher, 'Hyperbolische Typen im Arabischen', *Gesammelte Schriften*, III. 33–49.

world'.[83] In another Tradition: 'Whoever says so, his sins are forgiven even if he is a deserter from the march [of the army]'.[84]

Ḥudhayfa said, 'I had a stinging tongue against my family, and I said, "O Emissary of God, I fear that my tongue may bring me to Hell". The Prophet (may God bless him and grant him peace) said, "How far you are from asking for forgiveness! Verily I ask God for forgiveness a hundred times daily" '.[85]

ᶜĀ'isha (may God be pleased with her) said, 'The Emissary of God (may God bless him and grant him peace) said to me, "If you have committed a sin, ask God for forgiveness and repent to Him. Verily repentance of sin means contrition [*nadam*] and asking for forgiveness [*istighfār*]" '.[86]

The Emissary of God (may God bless him and grant him peace) used to say in his prayer for forgiveness, 'O God, forgive me my mistake, my ignorance and my intemperance in my affairs, and what You know better than I. O God, forgive me my flippancy and my over-seriousness [*jidd*], my error, my [imperfect] intention, and anything like these I may have. O God, forgive me what I did in the past and what I shall do in the future, what I did in secret and what I did in public, and what You know better than I. You are the Hastener [*muqaddim*] and the Postponer [*mu'akhkhir*]; You are Powerful over everything'.[87]

ᶜAlī (may God be pleased with him) said, 'I was such a man that, when I heard a Tradition from the Emissary of God (may God bless him and grant him peace), God made me profit by what He wished to make me profit by, and that when one of his Companions told me a Tradition, I asked him to swear and, upon his swearing, I trusted him. Once Abū Bakr—and he was veracious—told me a Tradition, and said, "I heard the Emissary of God (may God bless him and grant him peace) saying, 'Whoever commits a sin, and performs the ritual purification well, and proceeds to offer a prayer of two *rakᶜas*[A] and asks God for forgiveness, God will forgive him' ".[88] Then Abū Bakr recited the Word of God: *Those who, when they have committed a vile deed or wronged themselves . . .*'[89]

Abū Hurayra related that the Prophet (may God bless him and grant him peace) said, 'Verily when a believer commits a sin, he gets a black spot in his heart. If he repents and avoids [any further] sin and asks for forgiveness, then his heart is purified from it. If, however, further sins are committed, the spot increases until it completely covers his heart'. And that is the 'rust' [*rān*] which God mentioned in His Book: *Nay, but what they have earned is rust upon their hearts.*[90]

Abū Hurayra (may God be pleased with him) related that the Emissary of God (may God bless him and grant him peace) said, 'Verily God will elevate the rank for the servant in Heaven, so he will say, "My Lord, why this [rank] for me?" and God will say, "By virtue of your son's prayer for forgiveness on your behalf" '.[91]

ᶜĀ'isha (may God be pleased with her) related that the Emissary of God (may God bless him and grant him peace) said, 'O God, make me one of those who rejoice when they have done a good deed, and ask for forgiveness when they have done an evil deed!'[92]

The Emissary of God (may God bless him and grant him peace) said, 'When a man commits a sin and says, "O God, forgive me!" God says, "My servant has committed a sin. But he knows that he has a Lord Who takes off the sin and forgives it. O My servant, do what you want. For I have already forgiven you!" '[93]

[A] A unit or cycle of the Muslim ritual prayer which consists of standing (*qiyām*), bowing (*rukūᶜ*), two prostrations (*sujūd*), and sitting (*julūs*), together with the proper invocations, supplications, and inner attitude. For more details and illustrations, see Calverley, 16–8; Lane, *Manners and Customs*, 78–9.

He said (may God bless him and grant him peace), 'He who asks for forgiveness is not a persistent sinner even though he come back [to sin] seventy times a day'.[94]

He said (may God bless him and grant him peace), 'A man who has never done good looks up toward heaven and says, "Verily I have a Lord. My Lord, forgive me!" and then God says, "I have already forgiven you" '.[95]

He said (may God bless him and grant him peace), 'If a man commits a sin, but knows that God is watching, then God forgives him, even if he does not ask for forgiveness'.[96]

He said (may God bless him and grant him peace), 'God says, "O My servants, you are all sinners except him whom I have pardoned. So ask Me for forgiveness, and I will forgive you. Whosoever knows that I am the Possessor of the power to forgive him, I will forgive him, and I do not mind [doing so]" '.[97]

He said (may God bless him and grant him peace), 'If a man says, "Glory be to You! I wronged myself and committed evil. Forgive me! Verily no one forgives sins but You", his sins are forgiven, even if they are [as numerous] as the tracks of ants'.[98]

It is related that the best prayer for forgiveness is this: 'O God, You are my Lord, and I am Your servant. You have created me. I am observing my covenant and promise to You[A] as much as I can. I take refuge with You from the evil which I have committed. I acknowledge to You Your favour upon me, and I acknowledge to myself my sins. I have wronged myself, and I have confessed my sin. So forgive me my sins—those I have committed and those I shall commit. Verily no one forgives sins except You'.[B] [99]

[A] As to the meaning of the ᶜ*ahd* (and *wa*ᶜ*d*) in this context, the ᶜ*ahd* on the part of man, it is said, is his *tahlīl* and his obedience to God; and on the part of God it is to bestow salvation in the next world (Zabīdī, v. 61; Padwick, 129–30; Lane, *Lexicon*, 2183).

[B] This is the famous prayer for forgiveness (*sayyid al-istighfār*) (Zabīdī, v. 60–61).

Chapter Two

From the Narratives

Khālid ibn Maʿdān said, 'God says, "My servants who are dearest to Me are those who love one another with My love and whose hearts remain attached to the mosque, and those who ask for forgiveness at daybreak. They are such people whom, when I want to punish the people on earth, I remember and leave alone, and from whom I turn aside the punishment" '.

Qatāda (may God show him His mercy) said, 'The Qur'ān shows you your disease and your medicine. Your disease is sin and your medicine is praying for forgiveness'.

ʿAlī (may God ennoble his face) said, 'I wonder about a man who perishes, while he has a remedy'. On being asked, 'What is it?' he said, 'It is praying for forgiveness'.

He used to say, 'God (Glorified is He!) never inspired a man with praying for forgiveness when He meant to punish him'.

Al-Fuḍayl said, 'The meaning of the word of the servant: "I ask God for forgiveness" is "Raise me up [*aqulnī*] [from my sins]" '.[A]

One of the learned said, 'Man is between sin and grace. Nothing is good for these [two] but the praise [of God] and praying for forgiveness'.

Al-Rabīʿ ibn Khuthaym (may God show him His mercy) said, 'Let not any of you say, "I ask God for forgiveness and I turn to Him in repentance", for it is a sin and a lie, if he does not really do so. Rather let him say, "O God, forgive me, and relent towards me!" '

Al-Fuḍayl (may God show him His mercy) said, 'The prayer for forgiveness without any real commitment [*bilā iqlāʿ*] is the repentance of the liars'.

Rābiʿa al-ʿAdawīya (may God show her His mercy) said,

[A] Cf. Zabīdī, v. 61.

'Our prayer for forgiveness needs many prayers for forgiveness'.[A]

One of the philosophers said, 'He who prays for forgiveness before contrition [*nadam*] mocks God without being aware of it'.

A bedouin who was holding on to the curtains of the Kaᶜba was overheard saying, 'O God, verily I am asking for forgiveness despite all my persistence in vileness. It is really impossible for me to give up asking for forgiveness due to my knowledge of Your generosity in forgiving. How often You show love to me with Your favours in spite of Your independence of me! How often I make you angry with my sins in spite of my need of You! O You Who fulfil what You promise! You Who pardon what You threaten! Let my great sin enter into Your great pardon. O Most Merciful of the merciful!'

Abū ᶜAbd Allāh al-Warrāq said, 'If you have sins as numerous as drops [of rain] and the foam of the sea, they will be wiped off from you, if God (Exalted is He!) wills, when you sincerely supplicate unto your Lord as follows: "O God, verily I ask You for forgiveness for every sin which I once repented of to You, but which I returned to again. I ask You for forgiveness for every promise that I made to You from my own part, but that I did not fulfil for You. I ask Your forgiveness for every act that I wanted to do for the sake of Your Face, but that I mixed with something other than You. I ask You for forgiveness for every favour that You have bestowed upon me, but that I used for disobeying You. I ask You, O Knower of the Unseen and the Visible, for forgiveness for every sin that I committed in broad daylight and in the darkness of night, in public and in solitude, in secret and in the open. O Affectionate One!" It is said that this is Adam's prayer for forgiveness, or al-Khiḍr's'.[B]

[A] For Ghazali's own comment on this saying, see *Iḥyā'*, IV. 42 (K. al-Tawba, Bayān mā yanbaghī . . .).

[B] See below, 64 n.A.

CHAPTER THREE

Transmitted Prayers whose Authors and Circumstances [of composition] are Known and whose Use in the Mornings and Evenings and immediately after each Ritual Prayer is Desirable

To them belongs:

The prayer of the Emissary of God (may God bless him and grant him peace) after each dawn prayer of two rakᶜas:

IBN ᶜABBĀS (may God be pleased with him) said, 'Al-ᶜAbbās sent me to the Emissary of God (may God bless him and grant him peace). I came to him in the evening, and he was at the house of my aunt, Maymūna. He rose to perform the night prayer [there], and after he had performed the dawn prayer [*ṣalāt al-fajr*] of two *rakᶜas*—and before the morning prayer [*ṣalāt al-ṣubḥ*][A]—he said, "O God, I ask You for mercy

[A] Besides the five prescribed ritual prayers—the noon prayer (*ṣalāt al-ẓuhr*), the afternoon prayer (*salat al-ᶜaṣr*), the sunset prayer (*ṣalāt al-maghrib*), the night prayer (*ṣalāt al-ᶜishā'*), and the morning prayer (*ṣalāt al-ṣubḥ*)—which are obligatory (*farā'iḍ*) upon all Muslims, there are many supererogatory prayers (*nawāfil*). One of them is the type of prayer, called the voluntary prayer (*taṭawwuᶜ*), which is performed before and/or after the five prescribed prayers. Although there is some lack of agreement as to the nomenclature of these various types of prayer, Ghazālī is consistent in his own way, though not always. The dawn prayer (*ṣalāt al-fajr*) belongs to this voluntary type of prayer (Ghazālī, *Wajīz*, I. 53–4).

from You [*min ᶜindika*],[A] by which You guide my heart, by which You rebuild my integrity, by which You help me recover myself from confusion, by which You keep trials away from me, by which You restore my piety, by which You protect my interior and elevate my exterior, by which You purify my work, by which You give me honour, by which You inspire me with my right course, and by which You guard me against every evil. O God, give me a sincere faith and certitude, which admit of no return to unbelief. Give me the compassion by which I reach the honour of receiving Your grace in this world and the next. O God, I ask You for success according to Your Decree [*qaḍā'*], for the ranks of martyrs [*shuhadā'*], for the way of living of the happy ones [*suᶜadā'*], for victory over enemies [*aᶜdā'*], and for association with prophets [*anbiyā'*]. O God, I submit my need to You. Verily my intellect is weak, my artifice small, my work falls short, and I am in need of Your compassion. I ask You, O Protector of affairs, O Healer of breasts, to grant me protection from the punishment of the blazing flame and from the call to perdition, and from the trial of graves,[B] as You grant protection to the seas.[C] O God, the favour for which my intellect is too short, and for which my work is too weak, and which my intention and aspiration do not reach; the favour which You have promised to any of Your servants, or the favour which You bestow upon any of Your creatures—this favour I request of You and this favour I ask of You, O Lord of the worlds. O God, make us guides and guided, not astray and misguiding, in war against Your foes and in peace with Your friends. We love, through Your love, those of Your creatures who obey You, and we fight, through Your hostility, against those of Your creatures

[A] That is, on Your own initiative without any cause (Zabīdī, v. 63).

[B] See below, 69 nD.

[C] So that they may not blend and mix up with each other (Zabīdī, v. 63; cf. Q. LV: 19–20).

who disobey You. O God, this is the supplication and the answer belongs to You. This is effort [*jahd*] [on our side] and dependence is on You. *Verily to You we belong and to You we return.*[1] There is no might and no power save in God, the Exalted, the Magnificent, the Possessor of the strong rope [*al-ḥabl al-shadīd*] and the upright command.[2] I ask You for security on the Day of Threat and for Paradise on the Day of Eternity, together with those who are brought near [to God] and witnessing[A], and those who often bow and prostrate, and keep their covenants. Verily You are compassionate and affectionate, and You do what You will.[B] Glory be to Him Who wears might as a garment and speaks in it! Glory be to Him Who puts on grandeur and shows generosity in it! Glory be to Him Who Alone is qualified to monopolise glorification! Glory be to the Possessor of grace and favours! Glory be to the Possessor of might and generosity! Glory be to Him Who counts everything in His knowledge! O God, give me a light in my heart, a light in my grave, a light in my ear, a light in my eye, a light in my hair, a light in my skin, a light in my flesh, a light in my blood, a light in my bone, a light before me, a light behind me, a light on my right side, a light on my left side, a light above me, a light below me. O God, give me more light. Give me light. Make me light" '.[3]

The prayer of ᶜĀ'isha (may God be pleased with her):

The Emissary of God (may God bless him and grant him peace) said to ᶜĀ'isha, 'You must use the perfect prayer, whose use is general. Say: "O God, I ask You for all kinds of good, temporal and otherworldly, the good which I know and which I do not know. I take refuge with You from all kinds of

[A] The Beatific Vision.

[B] See above, 38 for a similar prayer.

evil, temporal and otherworldly, the evil which I know and which I do not know. I ask You for Heaven and the word and work which bring us thereto, and I take refuge with You from Hell and the word and work which bring us thereto. I ask You for the good for which Your servant and Emissary, Muḥammad (may God bless him and grant him peace), asked You, and I take refuge with You from that from which Your servant and Emissary, Muḥammad (may God bless him and grant him peace), took refuge with You. I ask You to bring to a right end, by Your mercy, the course of the things which You have decreed for me. O Most Compassionate of the compassionate!" '[4]

The prayer of Fāṭima (may God be pleased with her):

The Emissary of God (may God bless him and grant him peace) said, 'O Fāṭima, what prevents you from listening to what I bequeath to you? You may say: "O Living, O Self-Subsistent! By Your mercy, I beseech for help. Leave me not to myself even for the blinking of an eye. Improve my condition entirely" '.[5]

The prayer of Abū Bakr al-Ṣiddīq (may God be pleased with him):

The Emissary of God (may God bless him and grant him peace) taught Abū Bakr al-Ṣiddīq to say: 'O God, verily I ask You, by Muḥammad, Your Prophet, and Abraham, Your Friend, and Moses, Your Interlocutor, and Jesus, Your Word and Spirit; and by the Torah of Moses, the Gospel of Jesus, the Psalms of David, and the Furqān[A] of Muḥammad (the peace of God be upon them all!); by each revelation You revealed, or by each decree You decreed, or by each petitioner to whom You gave, or by each rich man whom You impoverished, or by each poor man whom You enriched, or by each strayer whom You guided; and I ask You, by Your Name which You revealed to Moses (upon whom be peace); and I ask You, by Your Name by which You disseminated the provisions of the servants; and I ask You, by Your Name which You laid upon the earth and this became established; and I ask You, by Your Name which You laid upon the heavens so that they were lifted up; and I ask You, by Your Name which You laid upon the mountains, so that they were made stable; and I ask You, by Your Name by which Your Throne was raised up; and I ask You, by Your Name, which is holy, pure, one, eternal, and unique, which is revealed in Your Book from You [and] from the illuminating Light [*al-nūr al-mubīn*]; and I ask You, by Your Name which You laid upon the day, so that it was light, and which You laid upon the night, so that it was darkened; and I ask You, by Your magnificence and splendour, and by the Light of Your Noble Face, to grant me the Qur'ān and the knowledge of it, and to blend it with my flesh, my blood, my ear, and my eye, and to utilize my body through it by Your might and Your power. Verily there is no might and no power save in You. O Most Compassionate of the compassionate!'[6]

The prayer of Burayda al-Aslamī (may God be pleased with him):

It is related that the Emissary of God (may God bless him and grant him peace) said to him, 'O Burayda! Shall I not tell you the words which God, if He wishes a good thing for a person, tells him and never lets him forget?' So [Burayda replied,] 'I said, "Yes, O Emissary of God" '. Then he said, 'Say: "O God, verily I am weak. Make me strong against my weakness in Your contentment. Take [me] firmly by the forelock to the good. Make Islam the utmost of my contentment. O God, I am weak. Strengthen me! Verily I am

[A] In ordinary speech *furqān* has the meanings of 'discrimination', 'revelation', and 'salvation'. In this case, it means the Qur'ān.

insignificant. Make me mighty! Verily I am poor. Make me rich! O Most Compassionate of the compassionate!" '[7]

The prayer of Qabīṣa ibn al-Mukhāriq:

When he asked the Emissary of God (may God bless him and grant him peace), 'Teach me some words whereby God helps me; I have reached old age, and so cannot do many things which I used to do'—the Emissary of God (upon whom be peace) said, 'Concerning your life of this world, say three times, when you have performed the ritual prayer in the morning, "Glory be to God, and praise be to Him! Glory be to God, the Magnificent! There is no might and no power save in God, the Exalted, the Magnificent!" When you say these words, you shall be safe from sorrow, black leprosy [*judhām*], white leprosy [*baraṣ*], and semi-paralysis [*fālij*]. As for your Afterlife, say, "O God, guide me from Your part. Pour upon me Your favour, spread upon me Your mercy, and bestow upon me Your blessings" '. He continued, 'Verily when a man persists in [invoking with] them and does not forget them on the Day of Arising, four doors of Heaven are opened for him and he may enter through whichever he likes'.[8]

The prayer of Abu'l-Dardā' *(may God be pleased with him):*

Abu'l-Dardā' was told: 'Your house has caught fire'—for a fire had already broken out in his quarter.[9] But he said, 'God would never do that!' He was told three times, but he continued to say, 'God would never do that!' Then someone came up to him and said, 'O Abu'l-Dardā'! The fire went out when it came near your house!' Abu'l-Dardā' said, 'I already knew that'.[10] He was then told, 'We do not know which of your two statements was more astonishing!' And he replied, 'I heard the Emissary of God (may God bless him and grant him peace) saying, "If one says these words in the daytime or at night, nothing will hurt him". So I recited them. They are: "O God, You are my Lord. There is no god but You. In You we trust. You are the Lord of the Glorious Throne. There is no might and no power save in You, the Exalted, the Magnificent. What God wills is, and what He does not will does not exist. I know that God is Powerful over all things, and comprehends everything in knowledge and counts everything in its number. O God, verily I take refuge with You from the evil of my soul and from the evil of every beast, whose *forelock You hold. Verily my Lord is on a straight path*" '.[11]

The prayer of the Friend, Abraham (upon whom be peace):

He used to say in the morning, 'O God, this is a new creation. Open it for me with obedience to You and close it for me with Your forgiveness and Your good pleasure. Bestow upon me therein a good deed which You accept from me, and sanctify it and double it for me. Forgive me an evil deed which I commit therein. Verily You are All-forgiving, Compassionate, Affectionate, and Generous'. He who has supplicated with this prayer in the morning has already offered the thanksgiving prayer of the day.

The prayer of Jesus (upon whom be peace):

He used to say, 'O God, verily I have become unable to repel what I hate and unable to obtain the profit of what I seek. The command has fallen into the hand of something other than myself. I have become a pawn [*murtahan*] for my action. There is no poor man who is poorer than I. O God, let not my foe gloat over my mishaps! Let not my friend work evil against me! Make not my misfortune be in my religious life! Make not the world my greatest concern! Let him not dominate over me who has no mercy upon me! O Living! O Self-Subsistent!'

The prayer of al-Khiḍr[A] *(upon whom be peace):*

It is said that whenever al-Khiḍr and Elias[B] meet in each season of the pilgrimage, they never separate without mentioning these words: 'In the name of God. *It is what God has willed!*[C] *There is no power save in Him.*[12] *It is what God has willed!* Every grace is from God. *It is what God has willed!* All good is in God's hand. *It is what God has willed!* No one dispels evil but God'. He who mentions these words three times every morning is safe from conflagration, drowning, and burglary, if God wills.[13]

[A] The name of a popular figure who plays a prominent part in Muslim legends. He is said to have become green through diving into the spring of life. There is no agreement as to whether or not he is a prophet. Some say that he lived in the time of Abraham, some in the time of Noah. His name does not appear in the Qur'ān, but nearly all the commentators agree that the mysterious person in Q. XVIII:59–81 is al-Khiḍr. Here he is represented as the companion of Moses. It is usually believed that he is still alive in the flesh and is still to be seen in sacred places, such as Mecca and Jerusalem, although some traditionists deny his existence. He flies through the air and meets Elias at the dam of Alexandria and makes the pilgrimage with him every year (T.P. Hughes, *Dictionary*, 272–73; A.J. Wensinck, 'al-Khaḍir', *SEI*, 232–35).

[B] Ilyās. A Biblical prophet, twice mentioned in the Qur'ān (VI:85, XXXVII:123–130). He is often confused with al-Khiḍr as is seen in the exegesis of the above-mentioned passage (XVIII:59–81). Sometimes they are supposed to be twins, not physically, but in their work and common activity. They go together to the fountain of life and drink from it. The two spend Ramaḍān each year in Jerusalem, observing the fast. They then make the pilgrimage to Mecca. After the pilgrimage, they clip each other's hair and depart with eulogies. Anyone who repeats these formulas three times morning and evening is immune to misfortunes such as theft, fire, drowning, and evil spirits (A.J. Wensinck, 'Ilyās', *SEI*, 164–5; Schaya, 'The Eliatic Function', *SCR* 1979, 15–38; T.P. Hughes, *Dictionary*, 108).

[C] *mā shā' Allāh*. For the syntactical explanation of this formula, see Zamakhsharī, *Kashshāf*, II. 485; for its popular usage, see Padwick, *Muslim Devotions*, 88.

The prayer of Maᶜrūf al-Karkhī (may God be pleased with him):

Muḥammad ibn Ḥassān said: 'Maᶜrūf al-Karkhī told me, "Shall I not tell you ten words: five for this world and five for the next? He who supplicates God with these words finds God (Exalted is He!) by them". I said, "Write them down for me". He said, "No; but I shall repeat them to you as Bakr ibn Khunays did for me. [Say:] 'God is enough for me in my religion. God is enough for me in my mundane life. God, the Generous, is enough for me in what distresses me. God, the Affectionate, is enough for me against him who oppresses me. God, the Stern, is enough for me against him who hurts me by evil. God, the Compassionate, is enough for me at death. God, the Merciful, is enough for me at the Inquisition in the Grave. God, the Generous, is enough for me at the Reckoning. God, the Beneficient, is enough for me at the Scales. God, the Powerful, is enough for me at the crossing of the Traverse. *God is enough for me. There is no god but Him. In Him do I trust, and He is the Lord of the Glorious Throne*' " '.[14]

It is related that Abu'l-Dardā' said, 'He who says seven times every day, "If they turn away, [O Muḥammad,] say: *God is enough for me. There is no god but Him. In Him do I trust and He is the Lord of the Glorious Throne*",[15] God will protect him from the matter of his next world which concerns him most, whether he be veracious or deceiving'.[16]

The prayer of ᶜUtba al-Ghulām:

He once appeared in a dream after his death and said, 'I entered Heaven by virtue of these words: "O God, O Guide of those astray! O Possessor of mercy upon the sinful! O Rescinder of the sins of the sinner! Have mercy upon Your servant, the one who is in serious danger, and upon the Muslims, all of them, and put us among those righteous and blessed *upon whom You have bestowed favour, such as the prophets, the veracious, the martyrs, and the righteous*. Amen! O Lord of the worlds" '.[17]

The prayer of Adam (upon whom be blessings and peace):

ᶜĀ'isha (may God be pleased with her) said, 'When God wanted to relent towards Adam (upon whom be peace), [Adam] circumambulated the House [of God] seven times—it was not built yet, but was a red mound [*rabwa ḥamrā'*] at that time—and then he proceeded to perform the ritual prayer of two *rakᶜas*, and said, "O God, verily You know my inward and outward. So accept my excuse! You know my need. So grant me my request! You know what is in my soul. So forgive me my sins! O God, I ask You for a faith which firmly grips my heart, and for a true certitude so that I can know that nothing shall befall me except what You have written for me, and I ask You for contentment with what You have ordained for me. O Possessor of majesty and honour!" Then God (Great and Glorious is He!) revealed to him, "Verily I have forgiven you. None of your descendants will come to Me and supplicate to Me with the like of what you supplicated to Me with, but that I forgive him, and remove his afflictions and sorrows, and take away his poverty from his sight, and do business for his sake behind each merchant, so that the world comes to him despite itself even though he does not want it" '.[18]

The prayer of ᶜAlī ibn Abī Ṭālib (may God be pleased with him):

He related that the Prophet (may God bless him and grant him peace) said, 'Verily God (Exalted is He!) glorifies Himself every day, saying, "Verily I am God, the Lord of the Worlds. Verily I am God; there is no god but Me, the Living, the Self-Subsistent. Verily I am God. There is no god but Me, the Exalted, the Magnificent. Verily I am God. There is no god but Me. I have not begotten, nor have I been begotten. Verily I am God. There is no god but Me, the Merciful, the All-Forgiving. Verily I am God. There is no god but Me, the

Originator of all things, and to Whom all things return, the Mighty, the Wise, the Merciful, the Compassionate, the King of the Day of Judgement, the Creator of good and evil, the Creator of Heaven and Hell, the One, the Unique, the Alone, the Eternal, Who does not take any female companion or child, the Unique, the Single, the Knower of the invisible and the visible, the King, the All-Holy, the Source of Perfection, the Trustful, the Protector, the Mighty, the Compeller, the Lofty, the Creator, the Originator, the Shaper, the Great, the Sublime, the Powerful, the Subduer, the Gentle, the Noble, the Worthy of praise and glorification, the Best Knower of the secret and [that which is yet] more hidden, the Able, the Sustainer, the Transcendent of creatures and creation."—God mentioned at the outset of each phrase "Verily I am God. There is no god but Me" (as we just quoted in the foregoing). So if one wants to supplicate with these Names, let him say, "Verily You are God. There is no god but You" and so forth. If he supplicates with them, his name is recorded among the humble prostrators [*sājidūna*] who are living close to Muḥammad, Abraham, Moses, Jesus, and the [other] prophets (may God bless them all), in the Abode of Majesty, and he has the reward of the worshippers in the heavens and on the earth. May God send blessing upon Muḥammad and every chosen servant!'[19]

The prayer of Abu'l-Muᶜtamir, that is, Sulaymān al-Taymī (may God be pleased with him) and his prayers for the glorification of God:

It is related that Yūnus ibn ᶜUbayd saw in a dream a man who was one of those killed as a martyr in the Byzantine territory, and asked [him], 'What is the most meritorious of the acts you saw there?' The man replied, 'I saw at a certain place the words of glorification of Abu'l-Muᶜtamir [coming] from God (Great and Glorious is He!) and they went like this: "Glory be to God! Praise be to God! There is no god but God. God is most great. There is no might and no power save in God, the Exalted, the Magnificent. This be as numerous as the number of what He created and the number of what He is creating, and this be as heavy as the weight of what He created and the weight of what He is creating; and this be as full as the expanse of what He created and as full as the expanse of what He is creating and as full as the expanse of His heavens and as full as the expanse of His earth and its like and its doubles; and this be as numerous as His creatures and as heavy as the weight of His Throne and as far-reaching as His mercy and the ink of His Words and as extensive as His good pleasure until He is well-pleased and when He is well-pleased, and this be as numerous as the number of the invocations His servants invoked in the whole past and the number of the invocations they will invoke in the remaining span of time, each year, each month, each week, each day and night, and each one of the hours, and in a single inhaling and exhaling of breaths, and in one of the eternities, from eternity to eternity, the eternity of this world and the eternity of the next world, and in the span of time longer than this, the beginning of which does not come to cease and the end of which does not run out" '.[20]

The prayer of Ibrāhīm ibn Adham (may God be pleased with him):

Ibrāhīm ibn Bashshār, his servant, related that he used to say this prayer every Friday, morning and night: 'Welcome to the day of abundance, the new morning, the scribe, and the witness! This day is a festive day. Write for us in it what we say in the name of God, the Praiseworthy, the Glorious, the Exalted, the Affectionate, and the Doer of what He wishes in His creation. I have entered upon the morning, with faith in God, with belief in the Meeting with God, confessing His

Proof, seeking forgiveness of my sin, bowing down before the lordship of God, denying divinity to any but God, being in need of God, trusting in God, and turning repentantly to God. I testify to God, His angels, His prophets, His messengers, the carriers[A] of His Throne, those whom He created and those whom He is creating, that He is God, beside Whom there is no god, Who is alone and has no associate, and that Muḥammad (may God bless him and grant him peace) is His servant and Emissary, and that Heaven is a reality; and Hell is a reality; and the Pool[B] is a reality; and the Intercession[C] is a reality; and Munkar and Nakīr[D] are a reality; and Your promise is a reality; and Your threat is a reality; and the Meeting with You is a reality; and the Hour is coming and there is no doubt about it, and that God will resurrect those who are in doubt about it, and that God will resurrect those who are in their graves. With [faith in] this I live and with it I die and with it I shall be resurrected, if God wills. O God, You are my Lord! There is no god but You. You have created me and I am Your servant, and I will observe my covenant and promise to You as much as I can. I take refuge with You, O God, from the evil I did and from the evil of every possessor of evil. O God, verily I wronged myself. Forgive me my sins, for no one forgives sins but You. Guide me to the best of human qualities, for no one guides to the best of them but You. Dispel from us their evil. For verily no one dispels their evil but You. Here I am intent upon Your service and upon aiding Your cause. All good is in

[A] That is, the angels.

[B] The Pool (*ḥawḍ*), at which on the Day of Resurrection the Prophet will meet his Community. Its members will be admitted to the drinking place and thereby acquire eternal bliss (Wensinck, 'Ḥawḍ', *EI*[2], III. 286).

[C] In the Qur'ān, the right of intercession (*shafāʿa*) is reserved only to God Himself and the angels (Cf. XXXIX:44; XLII:5). Later it was admitted to the Prophet by *ijmāʿ* for grave sinners (Wensinck, 'Shafāʿa', *SEI*, 511–12).

[D] The two angels who examine the dead in the grave and, if they prove to be sinners or unbelievers, punish them until the Day of Resurrection, except on Fridays (Wensinck, 'Munkar wa-Nakīr', *SEI*, 411–12).

Your Hand. I belong to You. I believe, O God, in the prophets whom You have sent, and I believe, O God, in the books which You have revealed. May God send ample blessing and peace upon Muḥammad, the Unlettered Prophet, and upon his Family—the seal of my speech and the key to it—and upon His prophets and Emissaries, all of them. Amen, O Lord of the worlds! O God, bring us to the Pool of Muḥammad and give us from his cup a drink, thirst-quenching, pleasant-tasting and delicious, after which we shall never thirst again. Assemble us [on Doomsday] in his group, not as the ashamed, nor the violators of the covenants, nor the sceptics, nor the tempted, nor those against whom You are wrathful, nor those who are astray. O God, make me free from the temptations of this world and help me to obtain what You like and are well pleased with. Improve all my states of affairs for me. Strengthen me with the word which is firmly established in this life and the next. Lead me not astray, even if I commit a wrong. Glory be to You! O Exalted, O Magnificent, O Originator, O Compassionate, O Mighty, O Compeller! Glory be to Him Whom the heavens glorify with their wings! Glory be to Him Whom the seas glorify with their billows! Glory be to Him Whom the mountains glorify with their echoes! Glory be to Him Whom the fish glorify with their tongues! Glory be to Him Whom the stars glorify in the sky with the constellations! Glory be to Him Whom the trees glorify with their roots and fruits! Glory be to Him Whom the seven heavens and the seven earths and those who are in and on them glorify! Glory be to Him Whom each of His creatures glorifies! May You bless Yourself and exalt Yourself! Glory be to You! Glory be to You! O Living, O Self-Subsistent, O Omniscient, O Affectionate! Glory be to You! There is no god but You, Who are alone and have no associate. You give life and death, and You are living and never die. In Your Hand is good. You are powerful over all things'.[21]

CHAPTER FOUR

Prayers Transmitted from the Prophet and his Companions, with the *Isnād* Omitted and chosen from the Collections of Abū Ṭālib al-Makkī, Ibn Khuzayma, and Ibn Mundhir

IT IS desirable for the aspirant that every morning the most beloved of his daily offices [*awrād*] be supplication, as will be discussed in the *Book of the Daily Offices*.[A] If you are one of those who long for the harvest of the next world, and follow the pattern of the Emissary of God in prayer, then say at the beginning of your supplication after your ritual prayer:

'Glory be to my Lord, the Exalted, the Most High, the Bestower![1] There is no god but God, Who is alone; He has no associate; to Him belongs sovereignty and to Him belongs praise. He is powerful over all things.'[2]

'I am content with God as my Lord, Islam as my Religion, and Muḥammad as my Prophet' (three times).[3]

'O God, Creator of the heavens and the earth, and Knower of the invisible and the visible, Lord of everything and King of it. I bear witness that there is no god but You. I take refuge with You from the evil of my lower soul and the evil of Satan and his companions.'[4]

[A] *Iḥyā'*, I. 333–67 (*K. Tartīb al-awrād wa-tafṣīl iḥyā' al-layl*), that is, the tenth Book of Quarter I (see our Introduction).

'O God, verily I ask You for forgiveness and prosperity in my religious and mundane life, in my family and my wealth. O God, cover my faults and render me safe from fear. Forgive my offences and guard me on my front side and my back, on my right side and my left, and against what is above me. I take refuge with You from being surprised by evil from below.'[5]

'O God, make me not feel secure against Your ruse [*makr*].[A] Entrust me not to any other than You. Remove not Your cover from me. Let me not forget Your remembrance. And make me not one of the heedless.'[6]

'O God, You are my Lord. There is no god but You. You have created me. I am Your servant. I will observe my covenant and promise to You as much as I can. I take refuge with You from the evil which I have committed. I acknowledge to You Your favour upon me, and I acknowledge my sins. So forgive me, for verily no one forgives sins but You' (three times).[7]

'O God, heal me in my body; heal me in my hearing; heal me in my seeing. There is no god but You' (three times).[8]

'O God, verily I ask You for contentment with the Decree, for the pleasant life (*bard al-ᶜaysh*)[B] after death, for the bliss of seeing Your Noble Face, and for yearning for the Meeting with You without any distress of loss and without any misguiding temptation. I take refuge with You from wronging or being wronged, from attacking or being attacked, and

[A] Cf. Q. VII:99.

[B] Literally, 'the coolness of life'. According to Zabīdī, this means attaining to the Eternal Divine Manifestation which admits of no more veiling, and the advancement of the spirit to the abodes of the blissful and the stations of those brought near to God (Zabīdī, v. 76). Or it may simply mean deliverance from various trials after death until the Judgement, including the trial of 'heat and sweat' on the plain (*Iḥyā'*, IV. 497–8 [K. al-Mawt, shaṭr 2, Ṣifat al-ᶜaraq]; tr. Winter, *The Remembrance of Death*, 180–1).

from committing any offence or sin which You do not forgive.'[9]

'O God, verily I ask You for steadfastness in my affairs, and for [my] firm resolution in the right course. I ask You for thankfulness for Your favour, and for good worship of You. I ask You for a humble and sincere heart, for an upright character, for a veracious tongue, for an acceptable action. I ask You for the good which You know. I take refuge with you from the evil which You know, and I ask You for forgiveness of what You know. For verily You know and I know not. You are the All-Knower of the hidden worlds.'[10]

'O God, forgive me what I did before and what I shall do later, what I did in secret and what I did in public, and what You know better than I. Verily You are the Hastener and You are the Postponer. You are Powerful over all things, and are Witness to every hidden thing.'[11]

'O God, verily I ask You for a faith which does not subside, and for a wellbeing which is not exhaustible, and for the eternal joy of the eye, and for the companionship of Your Prophet, Muḥammad, in the highest Garden of Eternity.'[12]

'O God, I ask You for the good things, and for performance of good deeds, and avoidance of evil deeds, and for love of the unfortunate. I ask You for Your love and the love of those who love You, and for the love of every deed which brings me nearer to Your love, and I ask You to turn toward me and to forgive me, and to have mercy upon me. When You wish to try a people, take me up toward You without [my] being tempted.'[13]

'O God, by Your knowledge of the invisible and by Your power over creatures, give me life so long as life is best for me, and give me death when death is best for me. I ask You for fear of You in the unseen and the visible, and for the word of justice between the states of good pleasure and wrath, for the middle way between affluence and poverty, and for the joy of the Vision of Your Face and for the yearning for Your Meeting. I take refuge with You from the distress which is in loss, and from misguiding temptation. O God, adorn us with the embellishment of faith and make us both guiders and guided.'[14]

'O God, impart unto us the fear of You by which You protect us against disobedience to You, and impart unto us obedience to You by which You bring Your Paradise to us, and impart unto us the certitude by which You ease the afflictions of this world and the next.'[15]

'O God, fill our faces with ashamedness toward You, and fill up our hearts with fear of You, and set in our souls Your majesty by which You submit our limbs for Your service. Make Yourself, O God, dearer to us than all else. Make us more fearful of You than of anything else.'[16]

'O God, give uprightness to the first of this day and prosperity to the middle of it and a successful ending to the last of it. O God, give mercy to the first of it, grace to the middle of it and honour and forgiveness of the last of it.'[17]

'Praise be to God, before Whose majesty everything becomes humble, before Whose might everything abases itself, before Whose sovereignty everything is submissive, before Whose power everything surrenders itself! Praise be to God, on account of Whose awe everything is calmed, and by Whose wisdom everything is disclosed, and before Whose grandeur everything becomes servile!'[18]

'O God, send blessing upon Muḥammad, his family, his wives, and his descendants! Bestow grace upon Muḥammad, his family, his wives, and his descendants, as You have bestowed grace upon Abraham and his family in the worlds! Verily You are Praiseworthy, Glorious!'[19]

'O God, send blessing upon Muḥammad, Your servant, prophet and Emissary, the Unlettered Prophet, Your entrusted prophet! Grant him the Praiseworthy Station [*al-maqām al-*

maḥmūd][A] which You have promised him on the Day of Judgment.'[20]

'O God, set us among Your pious friends, among Your prosperous company and Your upright servants. Use us in accordance with Your good pleasure with us. Give us success in achieving the things which You love to proceed from us. Govern us in accordance with Your good choice for us.'[21]

'We ask You for all good, its beginnings and its endings. We take refuge with You from all evil, its beginnings and its endings.'[22]

'O God, by Your power over me, turn toward me; verily You are the All-Relenting [*tawwāb*], the Compassionate. By Your clemency toward me, forgive me! Verily You are the All-Forgiving [*ghaffār*], the Clement. By Your knowledge of me, be affectionate to me. Verily You are the Most Compassionate of the compassionate. By Your sovereignty over me, let me overcome my lower soul, and let it not govern me. Verily You are the Magnificent King.'[23]

'Glory be to You, O God, and praise be to You! There is no god but You. I committed an evil and wronged myself. Forgive me my sin. Verily You are my Lord. No one forgives sins but You.'[24]

'O God, inspire me with my right course. Protect me against the evil of my lower soul.'[25]

'O God, give me lawful sustenance, for which You do not chastise me. Make me content with what You bestow upon me, and cause me thereby to do a good action which You accept from me.'[26]

'I ask You for pardon and well being, true certitude (*ḥusn al-yaqīn*) and happiness in this world and the next.'[27]

'O You Whom sins do not hurt, Whom forgiveness does

[A] Cf. Q. XVII:79. The doctrine of the Prophet's intercession on behalf of his Community was established by *ijmāʿ* as we have mentioned before, and this Qur'ānic passage is quoted as one of the divine evidences for this (Wensinck, 'Shafāʿa', *SEI*, 511–12).

not diminish! Grant us what does not hurt You, and give us what does not diminish You![28] *Our Lord, pour out patience upon us. Receive us unto You as Muslims.*[29] *You are my Protector in this world and the next. Receive me to You as a Muslim, and join me to the righteous.*[30] *You are our Protector. So forgive us and have mercy upon us. You are the Best of Forgivers. Prescribe for us good in this world and the next. Verily we have turned to You in repentance.* [31] *Our Lord, in You do we trust and to You do we turn. To You is the journeying.*[32] *Our Lord, make us not a temptation for the wrong-doing people.*[33] *Our Lord, make us not a temptation for those who disbelieve. Forgive us, our Lord, verily You are the Mighty and the Wise.*[34] *Our Lord, forgive us our sins and our intemperance in our affairs. Make our feet firm, and help us against the unbelieving people.*[35] *Our Lord, forgive us and our brethren who preceded us in faith. Set not rancour into our hearts against those who believe. Our Lord, verily You are Merciful and Compassionate!*[36] *Our Lord, give us mercy from You, and prepare a right path for us in our affairs.*[37] *Our Lord, bring us good in this world and good in the next. Guard us against the punishment of Hell.*[38] *Our Lord, verily we have heard a herald calling to faith:*[A] . . . (up to His word:) *Verily You do not fail to keep the tryst.* [39] *Our Lord, blame us not if we forget, or commit a fault. Our Lord*[B] . . . . (to the end of the Sūra).[40] *My Lord, forgive me and my parents, and have mercy upon them both as they did bring me up when I was little.*[41] and forgive the believers, both men and women, and the Muslims, both men and women, both alive and dead.'[42]

'My Lord, forgive and have mercy, and overlook that

[A] The following passage is omitted: *Believe in your Lord! And we believed. Our Lord! Forgive us our sins, and acquit us of our evil deeds, and receive us unto You with the pious! Our Lord! Give us what You have promised us through Your Messengers, and abase us not on the Day of Arising!*

[B] The following passage is omitted: *Lay not upon us a burden such as You laid upon those before us. Our Lord! Give us no load that we have no strength to bear! And pardon us, and forgive us, and have mercy upon us. You are our Protector, so help us against the unbelieving people.*

which You know. You are the Mightiest and the Most Generous. You are the Best of the Merciful, and You are the Best of the Forgiving. *Verily we belong to God, and unto Him we do return.*[43] There is no might and no power save in God, the Exalted, the Magnificent. God is enough for us! And an excellent Protector! May God send abundant blessings and peace upon Muḥammad, the Seal of the Prophets, and upon his Family and his Companions!'[44]

Various examples of the refuge-taking, as transmitted from the Prophet (*may God bless him and grant him peace*):

'O God, verily I take refuge with You from avarice. I take refuge with You from cowardice. I take refuge with You from being thrown *back to the most contemptible life*.[A] [45] I take refuge with You from the temptation of this world. I take refuge with You from the punishment of the grave.'[46]

'O God, verily I take refuge with You from covetousness [*ṭama*ᶜ] which leads to disgrace [*ṭaba*ᶜ][47] and from coveting a thing which is not to be coveted, and from coveting a thing for which there is no hope [in attaining].'[B] [48]

'O God, verily I take refuge with You from knowledge which does not benefit, and from a heart which is not humble, and from a supplication which is not heard, and from a soul which is not satisfied. I take refuge with You from hunger (for what a bad bedfellow it is!); from perfidy (for what a bad friend it is!); and from sloth, avarice, cowardice, and decrepitude; from being thrown *back to the most contemptible life*; from the temptation of the Dajjāl[C] and the punishment of

[A] A reference to senility.

[B] See Lane, 1881–2.

[C] al-Dajjāl (the 'Deceiver'), sometimes called *al-Masīḥ al-Dajjāl* (the False Messiah); the Antichrist, who will appear at the end of time and rule the world through his deception, for 40 days or 40 years, before finally being slain by Jesus. His appearance is one of the signs for the coming of the Day of Judgement. It is also said that he is called *al-masīḥ* because he is 'one-eyed'. (A. Abel, 'Dadjdjāl', *EI*², II. 76–7; Hughes, *Dictionary*, 328–9.)

the grave; and from the temptation which is in life and in death. O God, verily we ask You for imploring, humble, and penitent hearts in Your cause. O God, I ask You for Your resolutions of forgiveness, and the causes of Your mercy, and for security against any sin, and for the booty which is in every piety, and for attainment unto Heaven and salvation from Hell.'[49]

'O God, verily I take refuge with You from stumbling into destruction [*taraddā*], and I take refuge with You from sorrow, drowning, and death [under a crushed house][A] [*hadm*]. I take refuge with You from dying while turning [my] back on Your cause, and I take refuge with You that I should not die in pursuit of the world.'[50]

'O God, verily I take refuge with You from the evil which I know and the evil which I do not know.'[51]

'O God, keep me away from detestable qualities and deeds, diseases and lusts.'[52]

'O God, verily I take refuge with You from harsh trial, affliction, ill luck, and the malicious joy of enemies.'[53]

'O God, I take refuge with You from unbelief, debt, and poverty. I take refuge with You from the punishment of Hell. I take refuge with You from the sedition of the Dajjāl.'[54]

'O God, verily I take refuge with You from the evil which is in my ear and my eye, from the evil which is in my tongue and my heart, and from the evil which is in my sperm.'[55]

'O God, verily I take refuge with You from the evil neighbour in the place of residence, for the neighbour in the desert moves from place to place.'[B] [56]

'O God, verily I take refuge with You from harshness, heedlessness, poverty, despisedness, and misery. I take refuge with You from unbelief, poverty, disobedience, affliction, hypocrisy, the evil qualities, scarcity of sustenance, vanity, and

[A] Cf. Zabīdī, v. 84 for this interpretation.

[B] The harm done by a neighbour is not so great in the desert because he stays in one place only briefly (Zabīdī, v. 86).

eyeservice. I take refuge with You from deafness, dumbness, blindness, insanity, black leprosy, white leprosy, and [other] mean diseases.'[57]

'O God, I take refuge with You from the withdrawal of Your grace, and the removal of Your protection, and from Your sudden revenge, and all Your displeasure.'[58]

'O God, verily I take refuge with You from the punishment of Hell and the trial of Hell, and from the punishment of the grave and the trial of the grave, and from the evil temptation of wealth and the evil temptation of poverty, from the evil temptation of the Dajjāl, the False Messiah. I take refuge with You from debt and sin.'[59]

'O God, I take refuge with You from a soul which is not satisfied, from a heart which is not humble, from a ritual prayer which is not profitable, and from a supplication which goes unheard. I take refuge with You from the evil of grief and the affliction of the heart.'[60]

'O God, verily I take refuge with You from the dominion of debt, the dominion of the foe, and from the malicious joy of enemies.'[61]

May God send blessing upon Muḥammad and upon each chosen bondsman in all the worlds. Amen!

CHAPTER FIVE

Prayers Transmitted for every Emergent Occasion

WHEN you wake up in the morning and hear the *adhān*, it is desirable for you to respond to the *mu'adhdhin*. We have already mentioned this[A] and also the prayers to be said on entering and leaving the toilet, and about the prayers of ablution in the *Book of Purification*.[B]

So when you go out to the mosque, say: 'O God, set a light in my heart and a light in my tongue. Set a light in my ear and a light in my eye; a light behind me and a light in front of me; and set a light above me. O God, give me light!'[1]

And say also: 'O God, verily I ask You by those who ask You, and by this walking of mine toward You. I did not set out with insolence, with frivolity, with hypocrisy, and with vanity. Rather I went out with fear of Your wrath and with desire for Your good pleasure. I ask You, therefore, to deliver me from Hell, and to forgive me my sins, for verily, no one forgives sins except You'.[2]

If you go out of the house for a need, say: 'In the name of God! My Lord, I take refuge with You from wronging or being wronged, from being foolish or being fooled.[3] In the name of God, the Merciful, the Compassionate. There is no might and no power save in God, the Exalted, the Magnificent. In the name of God, dependence is upon God'.[4]

[A] Above, 47, and *Iḥyā'*, I. 146 (*K. al-Ṣalāt*, bāb I, Faḍīlat al-maktūba).

[B] *Iḥyā'*, I. 124–45 (*K. al-Ṭahāra*), that is, the third Book of Quarter I (see our Introduction).

When you arrive at the mosque and are about to enter it, say: 'O God, send blessing and peace upon Muḥammad and his family! O God, forgive me all my sins, and open for me the doors of Your mercy!' Then step forward with your right foot first when entering.[5]

If you see a man selling or buying in the mosque, say: 'May God not make your business profitable!'[6] When you see a man calling in search of something missing [*yunshidu al-ḍālla*] in the mosque, say: 'May God not return it to you!'[A] This is the command of the Emissary of God.[7]

When you have performed the dawn prayer of two *rakᶜas*, say: 'In the name of God! O God, verily I ask You for mercy from You, by which You guide my heart . . .'(up to the end of the prayer),[8] as is transmitted from the Prophet (may God bless him and grant him peace), on the authority of Ibn ᶜAbbās (may God be pleased with him).[B]

When you bow down, say during your bowing: 'O God, to You I bow down; to You I humble myself; in You I believe; to You I surrender myself; to You I entrust myself. You are my Lord! Humble are my ear, my eye, my brain, my bone, and my nerve. What my feet hold belongs to God, the Lord of the worlds'.[9] And if you like, say three times 'Glory be to my Lord, the Magnificent!'[10] or 'All-Praiseworthy, All-Holy is the Lord of the Angels and the Spirit!'[11]

When you raise your head from the bowing, say: 'God hearkens unto him who praises Him. Our Lord, to You belongs praise[12] to the fullness of the heavens and the earth, and

[A] We also find some apparently irreconcilable statements quoted by Tirmidhī to the effect that buying and selling in mosques is allowed by some jurists (*ahl al-ᶜilm*). This prohibition is immediately followed by another prohibition to the effect that people must not gather in a circle in the mosque before the Friday ritual prayer (Ṣalāt, 237). Abū Dāūd adds to the above condemnation of the *inshād al-ḍālla* the following explanation: 'For the mosques are not built for that' (*Sunan*, Ṣalāt, 164).

[B] See above, 57–9.

to the fullness of anything You decree hereafter![13] The Worthy of praise and glory, the Most Deserving of what the servant praises! Each of us is a servant to You. No one holds back what You give and no one gives what You hold back; and no man's efforts may aid him at all against You'.[14]

When you prostrate, say: 'O God, to You I prostrate myself. In You I have faith. To You I surrender myself. My face is prostrated to Him Who created it and shaped its forms and made the openings in it for the ear and eye. *Blessed be God, the Best of creators*![15] O God, to You my body and my thought are prostrate, and in You my heart believes. I acknowledge Your grace upon me and I acknowledge my sin—and this is what I have incurred upon myself. So forgive me. Verily no one forgives sins but You'.[16] Or you may say three times: 'Glory be to my Lord, the Most Exalted!'[17]

When you have finished a ritual prayer, say: 'O God, You are the Source of Security [*salām*], and from You is security. Blessed be You! O Possessor of Majesty and Honour!'[18] And you may supplicate with other prayers which we have mentioned.

When you stand up from a meeting [*majlis*] and want to make a supplication which atones for the idle talk which passed in that meeting, say: 'Glory be to You! O God, praise be to You! I bear witness that there is no god but You. I ask You for forgiveness, and I repent to You. I committed evil and I wronged myself. So forgive me; verily no one forgives sins but You'.[19]

When you enter a bazaar, say: 'There is no god but God, Who is alone; He has no associate; to Him belongs sovereignty and to Him belongs praise. He gives life and death, and He is living, and never dies. Good is in His Hand, and He is powerful over all things.[20] In the name of God! O God, verily I ask You for the good of this bazaar and the good of what is in it. O God, verily I take refuge with You from the evil of it and the evil of what is in it. O God, verily I take refuge with You lest I suffer a false oath, or a poor deal'.[21]

If you are in debt, say: 'O God, make me content with Your lawful things, instead of Your unlawful things, and make me rich enough with Your favour to dispense with anything other than You'.[22]

When you put on a new garment, say: 'O God, You have clothed me with this garment. To You belongs the praise! I ask You for the good of it and the good for which it is made. I take refuge with You from the evil of it and the evil for which it is made'.[23]

When you see an evil omen [*ṭiyara*] which you do not like, say: 'O God, no one brings good things but You, and no one takes away evil things but You. There is no might and no power save in God'.[24]

When you see a new moon, say: 'O God, make it rise and brighten [*ahilla*] upon us with security, faith, piety, well-being, true resignation, and success in what You love and are well pleased with, and protection against what You are displeased with. [O Moon!] My Lord and Your Lord is God'.[A] [25] And you may say:[26] 'A new moon of guidance and good! I have faith in your Creator'.[27] 'O God, verily I ask You for the good of this month and the good of [Your] Decree. I take refuge with You from the evil of the Day of Arising.'[28] Before this you pronounce the *takbīr* three times.

When a strong wind blows, say: 'O God, verily I ask You for the good of this wind and the good of what is in it, and the good wherewith it is sent. We take refuge with You from the evil of it and the evil of what is in it, and the evil wherewith it is sent'.[29]

When the news of someone's death comes to you, say '*Verily we are God's, and unto Him do we return.*[30] *Verily to our Lord we are turning.*[31] O God, write down his name among the

[A] Cf. Q. VI:76–7.

[number of] good-doers and put his book in the ᶜIllīyūn[A] and replace his loss among those bereft. O God, deprive us not of his reward. Subject us not to trials after he is gone. Forgive us and him'.[32]

You may say when you give alms: '*Our Lord, accept* [*it*] *from us. Verily You are the Hearer, the Knower*'.[33]

You may say when you lose something:[B] '*It may be that our Lord will give us in exchange what is better than it. Verily our Lord we implore*'.[34]

You may say when you begin an activity: '*Our Lord, give us mercy from You, and prepare for us a right path in our affairs*'.[35] '*My Lord, open my breast, and ease my task for me*'.[36]

On looking up to heaven, you may say: '*Our Lord, You have not created this in vain. Glory be to You! Guard us against the punishment of Hell*'.[37] '*Blessed be Him Who has set in heaven constellations, and has set among them a lamp,*[C] *and an illuminating moon!*'[38]

When you hear thunder, say: 'Glory be to Him Whom *the thunder glorifies and praises, and the angels do likewise from fear of Him!*'[39]

If you see a thunderbolt, say: 'O God, slay us not with Your wrath, and destroy us not by Your punishment! Forgive us before that!'[D](So related Kaᶜb.)[40]

When it rains, say: 'O God, [give us] a comfortable raining and a profitable raincloud![41] O God, make it a raincloud of mercy, and make it not a raincloud of chastisement!'[42]

When you grow angry, say: 'O God, forgive me my sin. Let the anger of my heart be gone. Protect me from Satan, the accursed'.[43]

[A] Cf. Q. LXXXIII:18–20. This is the Register where all the good deeds of the angels and Muslims are recorded; or it is the place where this Register is preserved. It is said to be in the Seventh Heaven, under the Throne (Suyūṭī, *Jalālayn*, 552; Zamakhsharī, IV. 232).

[B] In selling and buying (Zabīdī, V. 103).

[C] The sun.

[D] Cf. Q. XIII:13.

When you fear certain people, say: 'O God, verily we place You [as a safeguard] in their front, and we take refuge with You from their evils'.[44]

When you fight [in the *jihād*], say: 'O God, You are my supporter and protector. By virtue of You I will fight'.[45]

When your ear rings, invoke blessing upon Muḥammad (may God bless him and grant him peace) and say: 'May God remember him who remembers me with good!'[46]

When you see that your supplication is answered, say: 'Praise be to God, by Whose might and majesty good deeds are completed!' When it is slow in coming, say: 'Praise be to God, under all conditions!'[A] [47]

When you hear the *a<u>dh</u>ān* of the sunset prayer, say: 'O God, this is the arrival of Your night and the retreat of Your day. This is the voice of those who call upon You and the presence of Your ritual prayers. I ask You to forgive me'.[48]

When distress befalls you, say: 'O God, verily I am Your servant and the son of Your servant and the son of Your female servant. My forelock is in Your Hand. Your ordinance for me has been issued and Your decree for me is fair. I ask You, by each of Your names, by which You have called Yourself, or which You have revealed in Your Book, or which You have taught to any of Your creatures, or which You have assumed to Yourself in the knowledge of the invisible world, to make the Qur'ān the springtime of my heart and the light of my breast, the cure of my distress, and the disappearance of my sorrow and grief'. The Prophet (may God bless him and grant him peace) said, 'When sorrow befalls a man and he says this prayer, God never fails to disperse his grief and give him joy in its stead'. On being asked, 'O Emissary of God, shall we not learn it?' he said, 'Yes, he who hears it has to learn it'.[49]

When you find a pain in your body or in the body of someone else, apply to it the incantation [*ruqya*] of the

[A] See above, 40.

Emissary of God (may God bless him and grant him peace). When a man complains of an ulcer or a wound, he should put his forefinger on the ground and then raise it, and say, 'In the name of God. May the dust of our earth, with the saliva of one of us, heal our sickness, with the permission of our Lord!'[50]

When you find a pain in your body, put your hand on the aching spot of your body, and say three times: 'In the name of God' and say seven times: 'I take refuge with the might and power of God from the evil which I find and fear'.[51]

When grief assails you, say: 'There is no deity but God, the Exalted, the Magnificent. There is no deity but God, Lord of the Glorious Throne. There is no deity but God, Lord of the Seven Heavens and Lord of the Noble Throne'.[52]

When you want to sleep, perform the ablution first and rest on your right side facing the *qibla*. Then say: 'God is most great' thirty-four times, and then: 'Glory be to God!' thirty-three times, followed by 'Praise be to God' thirty-three times.[53] Then say: 'O God, verily I take refuge with Your good pleasure from Your displeasure, and with Your forgiveness from Your chastisement. I take refuge with You from Yourself. O God, verily I could not offer sufficient praise to You, even if I tried zealously; You are as You have praised Yourself'.[A] [54] 'O God, in Your name I live and die.'[55] 'O God, Lord of the heavens and the earth, Lord of all things and King thereof, *Splitter of the grain of corn and the date-stone*[56], Revealer of the Torah, the Gospel and the Qur'ān; I take refuge with You from the evil of every evildoer and the evil of every beast whose forelock is in Your hand. You are the First, and there is nothing before You. You are the Last, and there is nothing after You. You are the Manifest, and there is nothing above You; You are the Unseen, and there is nothing beyond

[A] For Ghazālī's own interpretation of this prayer, see *Iḥyā'*, IV. 85 (*K. al-Ṣabr wa'l-shukr*, shaṭr 2, Bayān ṭarīq kashf al-ghiṭā'). See also Goldziher, 'Über eine rituelle Formel der Muhammedaner', *ZDMG* 48 (1894), 95–100, especially for the phrase *aʿūdhu bika minka*.

You. Resolve my debts, and render me free from poverty.'[57] 'O God, verily You have created my soul and You shall take it unto Yourself. To You do its death and life belong. O God, if You cause it to die, forgive it, and if You cause it to live, protect it. O God, I ask You for wellbeing in this world and the next.'[58] 'In Your name, my Lord, do I lay down my side [on my bed]. Forgive me my sin.'[59] 'O God, protect me from Your punishment on the day when You assemble Your servants.'[60] 'O God, I have surrendered myself to You, turned my face toward You, and entrusted my affairs to You. I have entrusted my back to You for safety in hope and fear. There is no refuge and no escape from You except in Yourself. I have faith in Your Book which You revealed, and Your Prophet, whom You sent';[61] this should be your last supplication, for such was the commandment of the Emissary of God (may God bless him and grant him peace). Before this, say: 'O God, wake me up at the time You like best, and use me for the works You like best, which bring me very near to You and bring me very far from Your displeasure. I ask You, and You give to me. I ask Your forgiveness, and You forgive me. I supplicate unto You, and You answer me'.[62]

When you wake up from your sleep in the morning, say: 'Praise be to God, Who has revived us after giving us death, and to Whom we shall be resurrected!'[63] 'We have entered upon the morning, as have the sovereignty of God, the grandeur and might of God, and the magnificence and power of God.'[64] 'We have entered the morning on the disposition [*fiṭra*] of Islam, on the word of the *Ikhlāṣ*, on the religion of our Prophet, Muḥammad, and *the creed of Abraham, the upright, who was not one of the idolators.*'[65] 'O God, thanks to You we enter upon the morning and thanks to You we enter upon the evening. Thanks to You we live and die, and toward You is the journeying.'[66] 'O God, verily I ask You to send us to every good thing this day, and we take refuge with You from committing a sin this day, or from incurring a sin against a

Muslim, for You have said, *He it is Who slays you at night and knows what you have committed by day, and resurrects you therein, that the term appointed may be accomplished.*'[67] 'O God, Breaker of dawn, Maker of night as a time for rest, and of the sun and the moon for calculation;[68] I ask You for the good of this day, and the good of what is therein, and I take refuge with You from the evil of it and the evil of what is therein.'[69] 'In the name of God. *It is what God has willed! There is no power save in Him.*[70] *It is what God has willed!* Every grace is from God. *It is what God has willed!* All good is in God's hand. *It is what God has willed!* No one dispels evil but God.'[A] [71] 'I am content with God as my Lord, with Islam as my Religion, with Muḥammad (may God bless him and grant him peace) as my Prophet.' '*Our Lord, in You we put our trust and toward You we turn in repentance, and to You is the journeying.*'[72]

When the evening comes, one says the same, except [certain changes such as] 'We have entered upon the evening' and, besides this, one says: 'I take refuge with all the Perfect Words and Names of God from the evil of what God has multiplied and created, and from the evil of every evil-doer, and *from the evil of every beast You take by the forelock. Verily my Lord is on a straight path*'.[73]

When one looks into the mirror, one says: 'Praise be to God, Who has given moderation and uprightness to my person and has given nobility and beauty to the form of my face, and to Him Who has made me one of the Muslims!'[74]

When you have bought a servant or a young slave, or a riding animal, take his forelock and say: 'O God, verily I ask You for his good and the good of his inborn nature; and I take refuge with You from his evil and the evil of his inborn nature'.[75]

When you celebrate the consummation of someone's mar-

[A] The prayer of al-Khiḍr. See above, 64.

riage, say: 'May God bestow blessing in you, and upon you, and unite both of you in what is good!'[76]

When you pay a debt, say to the creditor: 'May God bless you in your family and possessions!' For the Emissary of God (may God bless him and grant him peace) said, 'The reward of a free loan [*salaf*] is praise and the payment [of the loan]'.[77]

These are the prayers which the aspirant must learn by heart, besides those given for such occasions as travelling, ritual prayer, and ablution, which we mentioned in the Books of the Pilgrimage, of Ritual Prayer, and of Purification.[A]

Should you ask: What is the benefit of supplication [*duʿā'*], while Preordination [*qaḍā'*] is irrevocable?—then you should know that the revocation of an affliction by supplication is itself a part of Preordination. Supplication is a cause [*sabab*] for the revocation of the affliction and the procurement of mercy, just as a shield is a cause for the deflection of an arrow and water is a cause for the growth of a plant on the ground. Just as the shield deflects the arrow and the two work against each other, so supplication and affliction work against each other. The acknowledgement of Divine Preordination does not require that one should carry no weapons—for God has said, *Take your precautions*[78]—nor that the earth should not be watered after dissemination of seeds, on the following assumption: if Preordination has been favourable to the plants, the seeds will grow; if not, they will not grow. In fact, the connection of causes with effects [*musabbabāt*] is the First Preordination [*al-qaḍā' al-awwal*] which is like *a quick glance of the eyes, or something nearer.*[79] And the arrangement of the particular effects for the particular causes by degrees and in accordance with the preordinated calculation [*taqdīr*]—this is Decree [*qadar*]. He Who decrees good does so through a cause, and He Who decrees evil decrees a cause for His rejections [of

[A] Respectively, the seventh, fourth, and third Books of Quarter One. (See our Introduction.)

good]. There is no contradiction between these matters to him whose inner eye is opened.

Furthermore, supplication has the same benefit as we mentioned with regard to invocation [*dhikr*]. For supplication requires the presence of the heart with God, and this is the apex of the acts of worship. Accordingly, the Emissary of God (may God bless him and grant him peace) said, 'Supplication is the marrow of worship'.[80] The propensity of human beings is for their hearts not to turn to the remembrance of God (Great and Glorious is He!) save in cases of need [*ḥāja*] and suffering from a calamity. Truly man, *once ill luck befalls him, is full of endless supplication.*[81] Need requires supplication, and supplication brings back the heart to God with humility and submission, so that there results the remembrance [of God], which is the noblest of the acts of worship. For this reason, affliction was assigned to the prophets (upon whom be peace), the saints, the virtuous people next [to them], and so on in descending order of their rank. For it brings back the heart to God in the state of neediness and humbleness, and prevents its oblivion [of Him]. Wealth, however, is a cause of arrogance in most cases. *Verily man is insolent, that he thinks himself self-sufficient.*[82]

The above are what we wished to cite from the totality of invocations and supplications. Verily God gives success towards good. The other prayers [to be said while] eating, travelling, visiting the sick, and so forth, will be dealt with in their proper places, if God (Exalted is He!) so wills. And dependence is upon God. Now the *Book of Invocations and Supplications* stands completed. God willing, it shall be followed by the *Book of the Daily Offices.* Praise be to God, the Lord of the worlds! May God send blessing and peace upon our master Muḥammad, and his family and Companions!

NOTES

Notes to Chapter One

1 Q. II:152.
2 Q. XL:60.
3 Q. II:186.
4 *aṣḥābih* (Z: *ṣaḥbih*).
5 *taslīm^{an} kathīr^{an}* (Z: *kathīr^{an}*).
6 Q. II:152.
7 Q. XXXIII:41.
8 Q. II:198.
9 Q. II:200.
10 Q. III:191.
11 Q. IV:103.
12 Q. IV:142.
13 Q. VII:205.
14 Q. XXIX:45.
15 Abū Nuʿaym, VI. 181.
16 Abū Nuʿaym, VI. 181.
17 Bukhārī, Tawḥīd, 43.
18 Ibn Ḥanbal, *Musnad*, V. 234; Ṭabarānī, *Kabīr*, XX. 166.
19 *yartaʿ* (TH: *yartafiʿ*).
20 Ṭabarānī, *Kabīr*, XX. 157.
21 Ṭabarānī, *Kabīr*, XX. 107.
22 Abu'l-Qāsim al-Iṣfahānī, *al-Targhīb wa'l-tarhīb* (ʿIrāqī, I. 265).
23 Daylamī, III. 454.
24 Bukhārī, Tawḥīd, 50; Muslim, Dhikr, 2.
25 *min jumlatihim rajul^{un} dhakara Allāh* (Z: *wa-dhakara min jumlatihim rajul^{an} dhakara Allāh*).
26 Bukhārī, Adhān, 36; Muslim, Zakāt, 91.
27 Ibn Māja, Adab, 53; Ibn Ḥanbal, VI. 447.
28 al-Bazzār, *al-Musnad* (ʿIrāqī, I. 266).
29 *yā ʿabdī* (TH and ZM: *ʿabdī*; Z: *ibn Ādam*).
30 Cf. below, 57n.
31 *ahl al-janna* (Z has *ahl al-dunyā*, which does not make sense in this context).
32 This sentence missing in Z.
33 Muslim, Dhikr, 38.
34 Ṭabarānī, *Awsaṭ* (ʿIrāqī, I. 266).
35 *ʿalā al-nabī ṣalla 'Llāhu ʿalayhi wa-sallam* (Z: *ʿalayya*).
36 Tirmidhī, Dhikr, 34.
37 Daylamī, *Musnad al-firdaws* (ʿIrāqī, I. 266).
38 Ṭabarānī, *Ṣaghīr* (ʿIrāqī, I. 266).
39 *ayy shay' taraktum ʿibādī yaṣnaʿūnah* (Z: *ʿalā ayy shay' taraktum ʿibādī yaṣnaʿūnah*).
40 Tirmidhī, Daʿawāt, 129; Ibn Ḥanbal, *Musnad*, II. 251.
41 Z adds here 'to Him belongs sovereignty and to Him belongs praise; He is powerful

over everything'. The Tradition is from Tirmidhī, Daʿawāt, 30.

42 Bukhārī, Bad' al-khalq, 11; Muslim, Dhikr, 27.

43 'eight' missing in TH and IH.

44 Muslim, Īmān, 46.

45 Abū Yaʿlā, *al-Musnad* (Haythamī, *Majmaʿ*, X. 82, 83).

46 *al-samāwāt al-sabʿ wa'l-arḍūn al-sabʿ* (Z: *al-samāwāt wa'l-arḍūn al-sabʿ*).

47 Ḥākim, I. 528.

48 Cf. Tirmidhī, Duʿā', 98.

49 Abū Yaʿlā, *al-Musnad* (Haythamī, II. 323).

50 Abū Nuʿaym, IX. 254.

51 *shirād al-baʿīr* (Z: *sharūd al-baʿīr*; Z also omits *ʿan Allāh ʿazz wa-jall*).

52 *yashrud ʿan Allāh* missing in Z.

53 Cf. Bukhārī, Iʿtiṣām, 2.

54 Cf. Q. XLVIII:26.

55 Cf. Q. II:256, XXI:22.

56 For this *ḥadīth*, which is a composite from various sources, see Zabīdī, V. 11–12.

57 Q. LV:60.

58 Q. X:26.

59 Ibn Ḥanbal, IV. 285, 304; Ibn Ḥibbān (*Iḥsān*, no.847).

60 *annahu qāla qāla rasūl Allāh ṣalla 'Llāhu ʿalayhi wa-sallam man* (Z: *annahu ṣalla 'Llāhu ʿalayhi wa-sallam qāla man*).

61 Ḥākim, I. 500.

62 Z: *wa-qāla ʿUmar raḍiya 'Llāhu ʿanhu*.

63 Ibn Māja, Dhikr, 5.

64 Muslim, Dhikr, 28; Bukhārī, Daʿawāt, 64 (with slight variation).

65 Bukhārī, Tahajjud, 21 (with slight variation). See also Ibn Māja, Duʿā', 16; Tirmidhī, Daʿawāt, 26.

66 Bukhārī, Tahajjud, 14.

67 Muslim, Masājid, 146.

68 Bukhārī, Daʿawāt, 65; Muslim, Dhikr, 28.

69 Judging from the context, I read *faqāl*, although all the texts have *faqult*.

70 *mādhā* (Z: *mā hiya*).

71 Daylamī, *Ma'thūr*, III. 474.

72 *al-suflā* omitted in Z.

73 Unidentified (Zabīdī, V. 14; ʿIrāqī, I. 269).

74 *awwal^an* (Z: *awwal*).

75 Bukhārī, Adhān, 126.

76 Ḥākim, I. 512.

77 As Zabīdī says, this Tradition was not transmitted by Ibn ʿUmar, but by (ʿAbd Allāh) ibn ʿAmr ibn al-ʿĀṣ (Zabīdī, V. 14; see also Tirmidhī, Daʿawāt, 59.

78 Z has *yanʿaṭif ḥawl al-ʿarsh lahu dawā ka-dawā al-naḥl yudhakkir bi-ṣāḥibih* rather than *yanʿaṭifna ḥawl al-ʿarsh lahunna dawā ka-dawā al-naḥl yudhakkirna bi-ṣāḥibihinna* as in ZM and the printed text of Ibn Māja. *Yudhakkirūna bi-ṣāḥibihinna* in IH and TH should be corrected to *yudhakkirna bi-ṣāḥibihinna*.

79 Ibn Māja, Adab, 56.

80 Muslim, Dhikr, 44.

81 Muslim, Dhikr, 12.

82 *fa-bā'i*^{ʿun} *nafsahu fa-mūbiquhā aw mushtar*^{in} *nafsahu fa-muʿtiquhā* (Z: *fa-bā'i*^{ʿun} *nafsahu wa-muʿtiquhā aw mūbiquhā*). The *ḥadīth* is from Muslim, Ṭahāra, 1.

83 Bukhārī, Tawḥīd, 58; Muslim, Dhikr, 30.

84 Tirmidhī, Daʿawāt, 127; Ibn Ḥanbal, v. 148.

85 Ibn Ḥanbal, II. 310.

86 Tirmidhī, Duʿā', 59.

87 Muslim, Zakāt, 52.

88 Ibn Māja, Dhikr, 20.

89 TH and IH have *b.sra*, but I adopt this reading according to the texts of Z and ZM.

90 Ibn Ḥanbal, VI. 371.

91 This Tradition was transmitted by ʿAbd Allāh ibn ʿAmr, not by Ibn ʿUmar (Zabīdī, v. 17; Tirmidhī, Daʿawāt, 25).

92 *shahida* (IH: *sh.dd*).

93 Tirmidhī, Daʿawāt, 20.

94 Muslim, Dhikr, 36.

95 *qul* is omitted in Z.

96 Bukhārī, Maghāzī, 38; Muslim, Dhikr, 45.

97 Muslim, Dhikr, 46.

98 *alā adulluka ʿalā*, which is omitted in Z.

99 Ḥākim, I. 21.

100 *rasūl*^{an} omitted in Z.

101 Ibn Māja, Duʿā', 14.

102 Ṭabarānī (Zabīdī, v. 19).

103 *lā sabīl lakum ilayh* omitted in Z.

104 Usually regarded as a *ḥadīth* of the Prophet. Cf. Ibn Ḥibbān, (*Iḥsān* no.819); Zabīdī, v. 19.

105 IH and Z have *wa-ākhiruhu yūjib al-uns wa'l-ḥubb*, but I read *wa-akhiruhu al-uns wa'l-ḥubb* in accordance with TH and ZM.

106 *wa'l-maṭlūb dhālika al-uns* (Z: *wa'l-maṭlūb huwa dhālika al-uns*).

107 *tadhkur ghā'ib*^{an} (Z: *yudhkar ghā'ib*).

108 *wa-in kāna takalluf*^{an}, which is omitted in Z.

109 *hiya al-nafs mā ʿawwadtahā tataʿawwad* (Z: *wa-qad qīl hiya al-nafs mā ḥammaltahā tataḥammal*). The saying is a famous hemistich by the poet al-Mutanabbī.

110 Ḥākim, IV. 325. Cf. Ghazālī, *The Remembrance of Death*, tr. Winter, 154–5.

111 Q. LV:27.

112 Tirmidhī, Qiyāma, 6.

113 Muslim, Imāra, 121.

114 *bi-asmaʿ* (IH: *asmaʿ*).

115 Bukhārī, Maghāzī, 8; Muslim, Janna, 91 (both with a slight variation).

116 *ṭuyūr* (Z: *ṭayr*).

117 Q. III:169–70.

118 *wa-li-ajl sharaf dhikr Allāh* (Z: *wa-li-ajl sharafihim bi-dhikr Allāh*).

119 *fa-innahu yurīduhā li-ḥayātih* (Z: *fa-innahu yurīdu amānatahu fi-'l-sharʿ*).

120 Z has *fi'l-sharʿ* in addition.

121 Z has this *ibnihi*.

122 Tirmidhī, Tafsīr Sūrat Āl ʿImrān, 18; Ibn Māja, Jihād, 16. Cf. *The Remembrance of Death*, tr. Winter, 129.

123 *ilayh* omitted in Z.

124 Z has this additional *sū'* (*al-khātima*).

125 *amr min al-dunyā* (Z: *amr al-dunyā*).

126 *fa-yaḥinnu ba*ᶜ*da al-mawt ilayh* (Z: *fa-yaḥyā ba*ᶜ*da al-mawt* ᶜ*alā dhālika*).

127 Bukhārī, ᶜIlm, 45; Muslim, Imāra, 150.

128 Q. IX:111.

129 Z has this *wa-lā ma*ᶜ*būd siwāh*.

130 Zabīdī quotes a Tradition: 'The most meritorious invocation is "There is no god but God". The most meritorious supplication is "Praise be to God!"' (See also Ibn Māja, Adab, 55.)

131 *dhakara fī ba*ᶜ*ḍ al-mawāḍi*ᶜ *al-ṣidq wa'l-ikhlāṣ* (Z: *dhakara dhālika fī ba*ᶜ*ḍ al-mawāḍi*ᶜ *ma*ᶜ*a al-ṣidq wa'l-ikhlāṣ*).

132 Tirmidhī, Janā'iz, 68.

Notes to Chapter Two

1 Q. II:186.

2 Q. VII:55.

3 Q. XL:60.

4 Q. XVII:110.

5 Q. LX:60. The Tradition is from Tirmidhī, Tafsīr Sūrat al-Baqara, 16; Ibn Māja, Duᶜā', 1.

6 Tirmidhī, Duᶜā', 1.

7 Tirmidhī, Duᶜā', 1; Ibn Māja, Duᶜā', 1.

8 Tirmidhī, Duᶜā', 5.

9 *al-faraj* (Z has *al-faraḥ*. Cf. Ghazālī, *al-Adab fi'l-dīn*, 75 [under 'Adab al-duᶜā'']). The Tradition is from Tirmidhī, Duᶜā', 115.

10 Q. LI:18.

11 Muslim, Musāfirīn, 168.

12 Z has this *li-banīh*.

13 Q. XII:98.

14 Attributed to the Prophet in Abū Nuᶜaym, IX. 320.

15 Tirmidhī, Duᶜā', 42.

16 Tirmidhī, Duᶜā', 44; Ibn Māja, Ṣiyām, 34.

17 *waqt al-saḥar waqt ṣafā' al-qalb wa-ikhlāṣih* (Z: *waqt al-saḥar waqt yaḥṣul bihi tamām ṣafā' al-qalb wa-ikhlāṣih*).

18 Muslim, Ṣalāt, 215.

19 Muslim, Ṣalāt, 212.

20 Muslim, Ḥajj, 38.

21 Abū Dāūd, Witr, 23; Tirmidhī, Daᶜawāt, 104.

22 Muslim, Imāra, 27; Bukhārī, Istisqā', 21.

23 Tirmidhī, Daᶜawāt, 117.

24 Tirmidhī, Daᶜawāt, 76.

25 Ḥākim, I. 536.

26 Muslim, Ṣalāt, 118.

27 Bukhārī, Maghāzī, 38; Muslim, Dhikr, 44.

28 Q. XVII:110.

29 Q. XIX:3.

30 Q. VII:55.

31 Abū Dāūd, Witr, 23; Ibn Māja, Duʿā', 12.

32 Q. vii:55.

33 Bukhārī, Daʿawāt, 19.

34 *jayyidīn* (Z: *khayyirīn*).

35 Q. ii:286.

36 Tirmidhī, Daʿawāt, 30.

37 Q. xxi:90.

38 Q. vii:55.

39 Daylamī, *Ma'thūr*, i. 251.

40 Bukhārī, Tawḥīd, 31; Muslim, Dhikr, 8.

41 Muslim, Dhikr, 9.

42 Tirmidhī, Daʿawāt, 65.

43 Q. vii:14–5.

44 Muslim, Jihād, 107.

45 Bukhārī, Daʿawāt, 22; Muslim, Dhikr, 90.

46 Ḥākim, i. 545.

47 Ibn Ḥanbal, *Musnad*, iv. 54. The Arabic of this prayer is: *subḥān Allāhi rabbī al-ʿalī al-aʿlā al-wahhāb*.

48 Cf. Tirmidhī, Daʿawāt, 64; Abū Dāūd, Witr, 23.

49 Q. ix:91.

50 *fa-lammā ḍajarū* (Z: *fa-lammā aṣḥarū*: 'when the people entered the wilderness').

51 Q. lxxxii:4.

52 Q. xx:7.

53 Q. xii:87.

54 Q. xxxiii:56.

55 Nasā'ī, Sahw, 47.

56 Ibn Māja, Iqāma, 25.

57 Tirmidhī, Witr, 21.

58 Nasā'ī, Adhkār, 40; Tirmidhī, Dhikr, 34.

59 Ibn Māja, Janā'iz, 65.

60 Ibn Māja, Duʿā', 14.

61 Bukhārī, Adhān, 8.

62 Ṭabarānī, *al-Muʿjam al-Awsaṭ*, (Zabīdī, v. 51).

63 Ibn Ḥibbān, (*Iḥsān*, no.909).

64 Dārimī, Manāsik, 96; Ibn Ḥanbal, *Musnad*, ii. 527.

65 Bukhārī, Anbiyā', 10; Muslim, Ṣalāt, 69.

66 Q. iv:80.

67 Q. ix:43.

68 Q. xxxiii:7.

69 Q. xxxiii:66.

70 Cf. Ibn Saʿd, *Ṭabaqāt*, i/i, 118.

71 Q. xxxiv:12.

72 For this incident see Ibn Saʿd, i/i, 113; also Bukhārī, Ṭibb, 55.

73 Q. lxxi:26.

74 Q. iii:135.

75 Q. iv:110.

76 Q. cx:3.

77 Q. iii:17.

78 Bukhārī, Tafsīr Sūrat 110, 1; Muslim, Ṣalāt, 52.

79 Abū Dāūd, Witr, 26; Ibn Māja, Adab, 57.

80 Bukhārī, Istighfār, 7.

81 Cf. Q. xlviii:2.

82 Muslim, Dhikr, 41.

83 Tirmidhī, Daʿawāt, 17.

84 Abū Dāūd, Witr, 26; Tirmidhī, Daʿawāt, 117.

85 Ibn Māja, Adab. 57.

86 Muslim, Istighfār, 54.

87 Muslim, Istighfār, 34.

88 Abū Dāūd, Witr, 27.

89 Q. iii:135.

90 Q. lxxxiii:14. The *ḥadīth* is from Ibn Māja, Zuhd, 29.

91 Ibn Ḥanbal, II. 509.

92 Ibn Māja, Adab, 57.

93 Muslim, Istighfār, 40.

94 Abū Dāūd, Witr, 26; Tirmidhī, Da[c]awāt, 106.

95 Ibn Abi'l-Dunyā, *K. Ḥusn al-ẓann* (Zabīdī, v. 59).

96 Ṭabarānī, *al-Mu[c]jam al-Awsaṭ*; *Ṣaghīr* (Haythamī, *Majma*[c], x. 211).

97 Ibn Māja, Zuhd, 30; Tirmidhī, Qiyāma, 48.

98 Bayhaqī, *K. al-Da[c]awāt* (Zabidi, v. 60).

99 Bukhārī, Da[c]awāt, 15. This *ḥadīth* is often transmitted with slight variations.

Notes to Chapter Three

1 Q. II:156.

2 Cf. Q. III:103, 112.

3 Tirmidhī, Da[c]awāt, 30.

4 Ibn Ḥanbal, *Musnad*, VI. 147; Ibn Māja, Du[c]ā', 4. Cf. *Qūt*, I. 17.

5 Nasā'ī, *[c]Amal al-yawm wa'l-layla*, 575; *Qut*, I. 17.

6 Abu'l-Shaykh ibn Ḥibbān, *K. al-Thawāb* ([c]Irāqī, I. 284); *Qūt*, I. 17.

7 Ḥākim, I. 527; *Qūt*, I. 18.

8 Ibn Ḥanbal, *Musnad*, v. 60 (abbreviated).

9 *qad iḥtaraqat dāruka wa-kānat al-nār qad waqa[c]at fī maḥallatih* (Z: *adrik dāraka wa-kānat al-nār waqa[c]at fī maḥallatih*).

10 *dhālika* (IH: *min dhālika*).

11 Q. XI:56. The *ḥadīth* comes from Ṭabarānī, *K. al-Du[c]ā'* ([c]Irāqī, I. 285–6); cf. *Qūt*, I. 19.

12 Q. XVIII:39.

13 'if God wills' omitted in Z. Cf. *Qūt*, I. 20.

14 Q. IX:129. *Qūt*, I. 20–1.

15 Q. IX:129.

16 *Qūt*, I. 19.

17 Repeated in Ghazālī, *The Remembrance of Death* (tr. Winter), 168.

18 *Qūt*, I. 22. Cf. above, 16 and 65–6.

19 Abū Nu[c]aym, IV. 34.

20 *Qūt*, I. 21–2 (with slight variation).

21 Cf. *Qūt*, I. 150–1.

Notes to Chapter Four

1 Ibn Ḥanbal, *Musnad*, IV. 54.

2 Bukhārī, Dhikr, 76; Muslim, Dhikr, 50.

3 Abū Dāūd, Ṣalāt, 36; Tirmidhī, Ṣalāt, 42; *Qūt*, I. 20.

4 Abū Dāūd, Adab, 139.

5 Abū Dāūd, Adab, 101; Nasā'ī, Isti[c]ādha, 60.

6 Daylamī, *Musnad al-Firdaws* ([c]Irāqī, I. 288).

7 Bukhārī, Daʿawāt, 15.

8 Abū Dāūd, Adab, 101; Ibn Ḥanbal, *Musnad*, V. 42.

9 Ibn Ḥanbal, *Musnad*, V. 191.

10 Nasā'ī, Sahw, 61; Tirmidhī, Daʿawāt, 23.

11 Bukhārī, Tahajjud, 1; Muslim, Musāfirīn, 199. Cf. *Qūt*, I. 23.

12 Ḥākim, I. 526.

13 Tirmidhī, Tafsīr, Sūrat Ṣād, 2, 4; Muwaṭṭā', Qur'ān, 40. Cf. *Qūt*, I. 24.

14 Nasā'ī, Sahw, 62. Cf. *Qūt*, I. 24.

15 Tirmidhī, Daʿawāt, 79; *Qūt*, I. 25.

16 Abū Nuʿaym, VIII. 282; *Qūt*, I. 25.

17 Cf. Haythamī, *Majmaʿ*, X. 96. Cf. *Qūt*, I. 25.

18 Ṭabarānī (Haythamī, Majmaʿ, X. 96).

19 Bukhārī, Anbiyā', 10; Muslim, Ṣalāt, 69.

20 Cf. Bukhārī, Adhān, 8. Cf. *Qūt*, I. 25.

21 Abū Nuʿaym (Zabīdī, V. 80). Cf. *Qūt*, I. 26.

22 Ḥākim, I. 520; *Qūt*, I. 26.

23 *Qūt*, I. 26–7.

24 Bayhaqī, *Daʿawāt* (ʿIrāqī, I. 282).

25 Tirmidhī, Daʿawāt, 69; *Qūt*, I. 27.

26 Ḥākim, II. 356; *Qūt*, I. 27.

27 Ibn Māja, Duʿā', 5; *Qūt*, I. 27.

28 Daylamī, *Musnad al-Firdaws*, (ʿIrāqī, I. 290).

29 Q. VII:126.

30 Q. XII:101.

31 Q. VII:155–6.

32 Q. LX:4.

33 Q. X:85.

34 Q. LX:5.

35 Q. III:147.

36 Q. LIX:10.

37 Q. XVIII:10.

38 Q. II:201.

39 Q. III:193–4.

40 Q. II:286.

41 Q. XVII:24.

42 Ibn Mājah, Adab, 2.

43 Q. II:156.

44 Ibn Ḥanbal, *Musnad*, VI. 315.

45 Q. XVI:70.

46 Bukhārī, Daʿawāt, 41.

47 *aʿūdhu bika min ṭabaʿin yahdī ilā ṭamaʿ* in IH should read *aʿūdhu bika min ṭamaʿin yahdī ilā ṭabaʿ*.

48 Ibn Ḥanbal, *Musnad*, V. 232.

49 Muslim, Dhikr, 73.

50 Abū Dāūd, Witr, 32; Nasā'ī, Istiʿādha, 61.

51 Nasā'ī, Istiʿādha, 58.

52 Tirmidhī, Daʿawāt, 126.

53 Bukhārī, Qadar, 13; Muslim, Dhikr, 53.

54 Nasā'ī, Istiʿādha, 46.

55 Abū Dāūd, Witr, 32; Tirmidhī, Duʿā', 74.

56 Nasā'ī, Istiʿādha, 44; Ibn Ḥanbal, *Musnad*, II. 346.

57 Nasā'ī, Istiʿādha, 36; Abū Dāūd, Witr, 32.

58 Muslim, Dhikr, 96.

59 Bukhārī, Daʿawāt, 39; Muslim, Dhikr, 49.

60 *wa-fitnat al-ṣadr* (Z and ZM: *wa-min ḍīq al-ṣadr*). The Tradition is from Muslim, Dhikr, 73.

61 Nasāʾī, Istiʿādha, 31.

Notes to Chapter Five

1 Bukhārī, Daʿawāt, 10; Muslim, Musāfirīn, 181.

2 Ibn Māja, Masājid, 14.

3 Abū Dāūd, Witr, 32; Ibn Māja, Duʿāʾ, 18.

4 Ibn Māja, Duʿāʾ, 18. Cf. above, 00.

5 Tirmidhī, Ṣalāt, 117; Ibn Māja, Masājid, 13.

6 Tirmidhī, Buyūʿ, 76; Ṣalāt, 237.

7 Muslim, Masājid, 79.

8 Tirmidhī, Duʿāʾ, 30.

9 Muslim, Musāfirīn, 201.

10 Abū Dāūd, Ṣalāt, 147; Tirmidhī, Mawāqīt, 79.

11 Muslim, Ṣalāt, 223.

12 Bukhārī, Adhān, 52; Muslim, Ṣalāt, 25.

13 Muslim, Ṣalāt, 194.

14 Muslim, Ṣalāt, 194.

15 Q. XXIII:14.

16 Muslim, Musāfirīn, 45.

17 Tirmidhī, Mawāqīt, 79; Ibn Māja, Iqāma, 20.

18 Muslim, Masājid, 135.

19 Nasāʾī, *al-Yawm wa'l-layla*, (ʿIrāqī, I. 293).

20 Tirmidhī, Daʿawāt, 35.

21 Ḥākim, I. 539.

22 Tirmidhī, Daʿawāt, 110.

23 Abū Dāūd, Libās, 1; Tirmidhī, Libās, 29.

24 Bayhaqī, Daʿawāt (ʿIrāqī, I. 294).

25 Tirmidhī, Duʿāʾ, 50.

26 This reading in Z is better than *yaqūl* in the other texts.

27 Abū Dāūd, Adab, 102.

28 Ibn Ḥanbal, *Musnad*, V. 329.

29 Tirmidhī, Daʿawāt, 48.

30 Q. II:156.

31 Q. XLIII:14.

32 Ibn al-Sunnī, 164.

33 Q. II:127.

34 Q. LXVIII:32.

35 Q. XVIII:10.

36 Q. XX:25–6.

37 Q. III:191.

38 Q. XXV:61.

39 Q. XIII:13; Mālik, *Muwaṭṭaʾ*, Kalām, 26.

40 Tirmidhī, Daʿawāt, 49.

41 Bukhārī, Istisqāʾ, 23.

42 Nasāʾī, *al-Yawm wa'l-layla* (ʿIrāqī, I. 295).

43 Ibn al-Sunnī, 134.

44 Abū Dāūd, Witr, 30.

45 Abū Dāūd, Jihād, 90; Tirmidhī, Daʿawāt, 121.

46 Ibn al-Sunnī, 55.

47 Ḥākim, I. 452.

48 Abū Dāūd, Ṣalāt, 38; Tirmidhī, Daʿawāt, 126.

49 Ibn Ḥanbal, *Musnad*, I. 391, 452.

50 Bukhārī, Ṭibb, 38; Muslim, Salām, 54.

51 Muslim, Salām, 67.

52 Bukhārī, Daʿawāt, 27; Muslim, Dhikr, 83.

53 Bukhārī, Daʿawāt, 11; Muslim, Dhikr, 80.

54 Nasā'ī, Taṭbīq, 47.

55 Bukhārī, Daʿawāt, 7; Muslim, Dhikr, 58.

56 Q. VI:95.

57 Muslim, Dhikr, 61.

58 Muslim, Dhikr, 60.

59 Nasā'ī, *al-Yawm wa'l-layla* (ʿIrāqī, I. 296); cf. Bukhārī, Tawḥīd, 13.

60 Abū Dāūd, Adab, 98; Tirmidhī, Daʿawāt, 18.

61 Bukhārī, Daʿawāt, 5; Muslim, Dhikr, 57.

62 Daylamī, *Musnad al-firdaws* (ʿIrāqī, I. 296).

63 Bukhārī, Daʿawāt, 7; Muslim, Dhikr, 58.

64 Ṭabarānī, *al-Muʿjam al-Awsaṭ* (ʿIrāqī, I. 296); Cf. Muslim, Dhikr, 58.

65 Q. II:135. The *ḥadīth* is from Ibn Ḥanbal, *Musnad*, III. 406.

66 Abū Dāūd, Adab, 101; Ibn Māja, Duʿā', 14.

67 Q. VI:60. For the *ḥadīth* cf. Tirmidhī, Daʿawāt, 94; Abū Dāūd, Adab, 101.

68 Mālik, *Muwaṭṭa'*, Qur'ān, 27; Daylamī, *Musnad al-Firdaws*, Nos. 1842 and 1989. Cf. Q. VI:96.

69 Abu Dāūd, Adab, 101.

70 Q. XVIII:39.

71 Ibn ʿAdī, *al-Kāmil fī ḍuʿafā' al-rijāl* (ʿIrāqī, I. 297).

72 Q. LX:4. The *ḥadīth* is from Abū Dāūd, Witr, 26; Tirmidhī, Ṣalāt, 42.

73 Q. XI:56. The *ḥadīth* is from Abu'l-Shaykh, *K. al-Thawāb* (ʿIrāqī, I. 297).

74 Ṭabarānī, *al-Muʿjam al-Awsaṭ* (ʿIrāqī, I. 298).

75 Ibn Mājah, Nikāḥ, 27; Abū Dāūd, Nikāḥ, 45.

76 Abū Dāūd, Nikāḥ, 36; Tirmidhī, Nikāḥ, 7.

77 Nasā'ī, Buyūʿ, 232.

78 Q. IV:71.

79 Q. XVI:77.

80 Tirmidhī, Duʿā', 1.

81 Q. XLI:51.

82 Q. XCVI:6–7.

APPENDIX I

PERSONS CITED IN TEXT – EXCLUDING PROPHETS

ʿABD ALLĀH IBN ʿAMR AL-ANṢĀRĪ, ibn Ḥarām ibn Thaʿlab ibn Ḥarām (d. 3)—28. A Companion (*ṣaḥābī*) of the Prophet. There is a tradition to the effect that when his son Jābir unearthed his body six months after his death, there was no corruption in it. (Ibn Ḥajar, *Iṣāba*, I. 341–342.)

ABŪ ʿABD ALLĀH AL-WARRĀQ—56. Unidentified.

ABŪ ʿAMR SHUʿAYB ibn Muḥammad ibn ʿAbd Allāh ibn al-ʿĀṣ al-Qurashī—14. The father of ʿAmr ibn Shuʿayb. A *tābiʿī* and narrator of Tradition, who transmitted traditions from his grandfather. (*Tahdhīb al-Tahdhīb*, IV. 56–7; Nawawī, *Tahdhīb*, 317.)

ABŪ AYYŪB, Khālid ibn Zayd ibn Kulayb al-Najjāri al-Anṣāri (d. *c* 52 [672])—14. A *ṣaḥābī*. It was in his house that the Prophet stayed first on his emigration to Medina. (*EI*^{2}, I. 108–9 [F. Lévi-Provençal, *et al.*].)

ABŪ BAKR al-Ṣiddīq (d. 13 [634])—52–3. The foremost member, next to the Prophet, of the earliest Muslim community. The first Caliph. (*EI*^{2}, I. 109–11 [W. M. Watt].)

ABU'L-DARDĀ' al Khazrajī al-Anṣārī (d. 32 [652/3])—8, 35, 62–3, 65. A *ṣaḥābī*. He was famous for his piety and strict observance of religious practices; a known authority on the Qur'ān and one of the few who collected the Qur'ān as it was being revealed. (*EI*^{2}, I. 113–4 [A. Jeffery].)

ABŪ DHARR, Jundub ibn Junāda al-Ghifārī (d. 32 [652] or 31 [651])—18, 19, 32. A *ṣaḥābī* and one of the earlier converts to Islam. He was noted for humility and asceticism, and was eager for knowledge and, it is said, matched Ibn Masʿūd in religious learning. (*EI^2*, I, 114–5 [J. Robson].)

ABU'L-ḤASAN—50. See ʿal-Shāfiʿī.

ABŪ HURAYRA al-Dawsi al-Yamānī (d. 57–59 [676/7–678/9])—10, 12, 17, 18, 20, 32, 34, 38, 53. A *ṣaḥābī* and the most prolific narrator of Tradition in spite of the shortness of his contact with the Prophet. He was particularly respected by the Sufis as one of the 'poor men', called *ahl al-ṣuffa* (see p.00 above, n.A). (*EI^2*, I. 129 [J. Robson].)

ABŪ MĀLIK AL-ASHʿARĪ (d. 3 [624/5])—18. There is no agreement about his *ism*. A *ṣaḥābī*. He was killed at the Battle of Uḥud. (*Tahdhīb al-Tahdhīb*, XII. 218–19.)

ABŪ MUḤAMMAD, ʿAbd Allāh ibn ʿAmr ibn al-ʿĀṣ (d. *c* 63 [682/3])—14. The grandfather of ʿAmr ibn Shuʿayb. A *ṣaḥābī* and a prolific narrator of Tradition. In contrast to his father, a famous general, he was a zealous searcher of religious knowledge. (Goldziher, *Le Dogme et la loi de l'Islam*, 116; Nawawī, *Tahdhīb*, 361–2.)

ABŪ MŪSĀ, ʿAbd Allāh ibn Qays ibn Sulaymān al-Ashʿarī (d. *c* 42 [662])—20, 35. A *ṣaḥābī* and an Arab general. He was appointed arbitrator representing ʿAlī at the Battle of Ṣiffīn (37 AH). He was also a scholar of Qur'ānic studies. (*EI^2*, I. 695–6 [L. Veccia Vaglieri].)

ABŪ MUṢʿAB SAʿD ibn Abī Waqqāṣ (d. 50 [670/1] or 55 [674/5])—20. The father of Muṣʿab ibn Saʿd, he was a famous Arab general and one of the oldest *ṣaḥābīs*. He was appointed by ʿUmar to be one of the six to choose a new Caliph. (*SEI*, 482 [K. V. Zetterstéen].)

Appendix 1

ABU'L-MUʿTAMIR, Sulaymān ibn Tarkhān al-Taymī (d. 143 [760/1])—67–8. A very pious traditionist. It is said that when he narrated the Prophetic Tradition his colour changed. He once became sick and wept; on being asked the reason, he said, 'I once greeted a Qadarite with a *salām*, and I fear the reckoning about it [on the Day of Judgement]'. (Zabīdī, v. 72; *GAS*, I. 285–86; Dhahabī, *Tadhkira*, I. 150–52.)

ABU'L-ṢADĪQ AL-NĀJĪ, Bakr ibn Qays (d. 108 [726/7])—43. A traditionist. (Ibn al-Athīr, *Lubāb*, III. 205.)

ABŪ SAʿĪD AL-KHUDRĪ, Saʿd ibn Mālik ibn Sinān al-Anṣārī (d. 74 [693/4] or 63–5 [682/3–684/5)—10, 20. A *ṣaḥābī* and a famous narrator of Tradition. (*Iṣāba*, II. 32–33.)

ABŪ ṢĀLIḤ al-Sammān al-Madanī (d. 101 [719/10])—10. A famous narrator of Tradition. It is said that al-Aʿmash transmitted a thousand traditions from him. (Zabīdī, v. 9; Dhahabī, *Tadhkira*, I. 89–90.)

ABŪ SULAYMĀN AL-DĀRĀNĪ, ʿAbd al-Raḥmān ibn Aḥmad ibn ʿAṭīya (d. 205 [820/1] or 215 [830/1])—41. A Sufi noted for his severe austerities and acts of self-mortification. He left a great number of his sayings. (Ibn Khallikān [de Slane], II. 88–89; Hujwīrī, 112–3.)

ABŪ ṬĀLIB AL-MAKKĪ, ibn Muḥammad ibn ʿAṭīya al-Ḥārithī (d. 386 [996/7])—41, 71. A famous Sufi and traditionist, leader of the dogmatic school of the Sālimīya in Basra. His chief work is the *Qūt al-qulūb*, which was studied closely by Ghazālī. (Ibn Khallikān, III. 20–21; EI^2, I. 153 [L. Massignon].)

ʿĀ'ISHA bint Abī Bakr al-Ṣiddīq (d. 58 [677/8] or 57 [676/7])—36, 52, 53, 60, 66. A favourite wife of the Prophet. She is often called the 'Mother of the Believers', and was also a prolific narrator of Tradition and an expert on Arab poetry. (EI^2, I. 307–8 [W. M. Watt].)

ʿALĪ ibn Abī Ṭālib (d. 40 [660])—52, 55, 66–7. A cousin and son-in-law of the Prophet and the fourth Caliph. Assassinated at Kufa. (*EI*^{2}, I. 381–6 [L. Veccia Vaglieri].)

ʿALQAMA, Abū Shibl ibn Qays ibn ʿAbd Allāh (d. 62 [681/2])—50. A Kufan *faqīh*, representing the school of Ibn Masʿūd. (*GAS*, I. 398; Shīrāzī, *Ṭabaqāt*, 58.)

AL-AʿMASH, Abū Muḥammad Sulaymān ibn Mihrān al-Kūfī (d. *c* 148 [765/6])—10. A traditionist and famous Qur'ān-reader. (*EI*^{2}, I. 431 [C. Brockelmann [C. Pellat]].)

ʿAMR IBN SHUʿAYB, Abū Ibrāhīm ibn Muḥammad ibn ʿAbd Allāh ibn ʿAmr ibn al-ʿĀṣ al-Qurashī (d. 118 [736/7])—14. A traditionist. Although he belonged to the generation subsequent to the *tābiʿīs*, many of them came to him to learn Tradition. (*Tahdhīb al-Tahdhīb*, VII. 48–55; Nawawī, *Tahdhīb*, 476–8.)

ANAS, Abū Ḥamza ibn Mālik (d. 91–3 [709/10–711/2])—34. One of the most prolific narrators of Tradition. His mother gave him to the Prophet as servant, and he remained in the Prophet's service until the latter died. He himself died at a very advanced age (97–107). (*EI*^{2}, I. 482 [A.J. Wensinck—J. Robson].)

AL-ASWAD, Abū ʿAmr (or Abū ʿAbd al-Raḥmān) ibn Yazīd al-Nakhaʿī (d. *c* 75 [694/5])—50. A cousin of ʿAlqama. He was also a follower of the school of Ibn Masʿūd. (*GAS*, I. 398; Shīrāzī, *Ṭabaqāt*, 58; Ibn al-Athīr, *Lubāb*, III. 220.)

ʿAṬĀ' AL-SALĪMĪ (d. 121 [738–9])—44. A man of extreme piety. It is said, though doubtful, that he did not raise up his head towards heaven out of his sense of shame before God. The text has al-S.l.mī rather than al-Salīmī; an error identified by Zabīdī. (Zabīdī, V. 47; Ibn Taghrībirdī, I. 287.)

AL-AWZĀʿĪ, Abū ʿAmr ʿAbd al-Raḥmān ibn ʿAmr (d. 157)—43. A noted *faqīh*, a main representative of the ancient

Syrian school of law. His *madhhab* was later superseded by the Mālikites in Syria and the Maghrib. (*EI*^{2}, I. 772–3 [J. Schacht]; *GAS*, I. 516–7.)

BAKR IBN KHUNAYS al-Kūfī—65. A pious traditionist of Baghdād. He was the teacher of Maʿrūf al-Karkhī (d. 200 [815/6]). (*Tārīkh Baghdād*, VI. 88–90; Dhahabī, *Mīzān*, I. 344.)

AL-BARĀ' IBN ʿĀZIB al-Awsī al-Anṣārī (d. 71 or 72 [690/1–691/2])—13. A *ṣaḥābi* and a devoted follower of ʿAlī (*EI*^{2}, I. 1025 [K. V. Zetterstéen].)

BILĀL IBN SAʿD, Tamīm al-Sakūfī (d. 122 [739/40])—43. The *imām* of the Damascus Mosque. His piety was compared to that of al-Ḥasan al-Baṣrī. (Ibn Taghrībirdī, I. 288.)

BURAYDA AL-ASLAMĪ ibn al-Ḥuṣayb—61–2. He took part in all the Prophet's campaigns after his acceptance of Islam after the Battle of Uḥud. Later he settled in Marw and died there some time in the reign of Yazīd ibn Muʿāwiya (60–63 AH). (*EI*^{2}, I. 1313 [K. V. Zetterstéen—W. ʿArafat].)

FĀṬIMA (d. 11 [632])—60. Daughter of the Prophet and Khadīja; wife of ʿAlī ibn Abī Ṭālib and mother of al-Ḥasan and al-Ḥusayn. (*EI*^{2}, II. 841–50 [L. V. Vaglieri].)

AL-FUḌAYL ibn ʿIyāḍ (d. 187 [803/4])—8, 45, 55. A converted highway robber and a famous ascetic. He studied Tradition under Sufyān al-Thawrī at Kūfa. The Caliph Hārūn al-Rashīd called him 'the Prince of the Muslims'. (*EI*^{2}, II. 936 [M. Smith].)

ḤABĪB AL-ʿAJAMĪ, Abū Muḥammad ibn ʿĪsā (d. 119 [737])—37. Of Persian origin, he was a disciple of al-Ḥasan al-Baṣrī. His asceticism and piety are proverbial. (Ibn al-Athīr, *Lubāb*, II. 124; Ibn Taghrībirdī, I. 283; Hujwīrī, 88–9.)

AL-ḤASAN AL-BAṢRĪ (d. 110 [728/9])—9. A learned traditionist, a famous preacher and ascetic of the Umayyad period.

One of the most important figures in the religious history of Islam. (*EI*^{2}, III. 247–48 [H. Ritter]; Massignon, *Essai*, 174–200.)

ḤUDHAYFA, Abū ʿAbd Allāh ibn al-Yamān al-ʿAbasī (d. 36 [656/7])—52. One of the older *ṣaḥābīs*. He was, together with Abū Dharr and Abu'l-Dardā', famous for asceticism, and was also one of those *ṣaḥābīs* who were called *ṣāḥib sirr al-Nabī*, because of their secret knowledge given by the Prophet. (Goldziher, *Le Dogme*, 274, n.77; *Iṣāba*, I. 316–17; Nawawī, *Tahdhīb*, 199–201.)

IBN ʿABBĀS, ʿAbd Allāh (d. 68 [687/8])—5, 34, 35, 57. A cousin of the Prophet. He was one of the great scholars, particularly as a Qur'ān-exegete, of the earliest period of Islam. (*EI*^{2}, I. 40–1 [L. Veccia Vaglieri].)

IBN KHUZAYMA, Abū Bakr Muḥammad ibn Isḥāq ibn al-Mughīra al-Sulamī al-Nīsābūrī (d. 311 [923/4])—71. A celebrated theologian and Shāfiʿite traditionist. He is said to have written more than 140 books. Among them are: *Bayān sha'n al-duʿā' wa-tafsīr al-adʿiya al-ma'thūra ʿan al-Nabī*; *Kitāb al-tawḥīd wa-ithbāt ṣifāt al-Rabb* (*GAS*, I. 601); *al-Mukhtaṣar al-ṣaḥīḥ* (Kaḥḥāla, *Muʿjam al-mu'allifīn*, IX. 39–40); *Ṣaḥīḥ Ibn Khuzayma* (printed in Beirut, n.d.). (See also *GAL*, I. 193; *GALS*, I. 345; Dhahabī, *Tadhkira*, II. 720–31.)

IBN MASʿŪD, Abū ʿAbd al-Raḥmān ʿAbd Allāh al-Hudhalī (d. 32 [652/3] or 33 [653/4])—40, 50. One of the earliest converts to Islam. Though of humble origin, he was fortunate enough to be on close terms with the Prophet and to become authoritative on Qur'ān-reading, exegesis, legal matters, and Tradition. (*EI*^{2}, III. 873–75 [J.-C. Vadet]; *GAS*, I. 398.)

IBN AL-MUBĀRAK, Abū ʿAbd al-Raḥmān ʿAbd Allāh ibn Wāḍiḥ al-Ḥanẓalī al-Marwazī (d. 181 [797/8])—45. A celebrated *faqīh* and ascetic. He travelled widely and learned the *Muwaṭṭa'* from Mālik ibn Anas himself in Medina. (Ibn Khallikān, II. 12–3; Zabīdī, I. 208–9; ʿAṭṭār, 124–8.)

IBN MUNDHIR, Abū Bakr Muḥammad ibn Ibrāhīm al-Mundhirī al-Nīsābūrī (d. 309 [921/2] or 310 [922/3] or 318 [930/1])—71. A *faqīh* of great learning. Besides the books on *fiqh* and *tafsīr* listed by F.Sezgin (*GAS*, I. 495–96), Ḥājjī Khalīfa mentions a book entitled *Jāmiʿ al-adhkār* (*Kashf*, II. 500), from which Ghazālī may have quoted. (See also *GAL*, I. 180; *GALS*, I. 306; Ibn Khallikān, II. 612–13; Shīrāzī, *Ṭabaqāt*, 89.)

IBN ʿUMAR, ʿAbd Allāh (d. 73 [693/4])—17, 20. A Companion of the Prophet who is remembered as one of the foremost legal scholars of early Islam. (EI^2, I. 53–4 [L. Veccia Vaglieri].)

IBRĀHĪM IBN ADHAM, Abū Isḥāq ibn Manṣūr ibn Yazīd (d. *c* 160 [776/7])—68–70. A famous ascetic from Balkh. His dramatic conversion, reminiscent of that of Buddha, is well-known. (*SEI*, 155–6 [R.A. Nicholson]; Qushayrī, I. 51–53; Hujwīrī, 103–5.)

IBRĀHĪM IBN BASHSHĀR—68. Unidentified.

JĀBIR, Abū ʿAbd Allāh ibn ʿAbd Allāh al-Anṣārī (d. 68 [687/8] or 73 [692/3] or 78 [697/8])—19, 28, 34. A *ṣaḥābī* and prolific narrator of Tradition. He died at Medina. (Nawawī, *Tahdhīb*, 184–6.)

KAʿB AL-AḤBĀR, Abū Isḥāq ibn Mātiʿ al-Ḥimyarī (d. 32 [652/3] or 34 [654/5])—41, 85. 'The Rabbi Kaʿb'—a Jewish convert of Yemen, who became a Muslim in the Caliphate of Abū Bakr or ʿUmar. He was the oldest authority for the Jewish-Muslim traditions in Islam. (EI^2, IV. 316–7 [M. Schmitz].)

KHĀLID IBN MAʿDĀN al-Kilāʿī (d. 145 [762/3])—55. An eminent *tābiʿī* and *faqīh*. He is said to have recited *Subḥāna'llāh* four thousand times a day. (Zabīdī V. 61.)

MAʿRŪF AL-KARKHĪ, Abū Maḥfūẓ ibn Fīrūz (d. 200 [815/6] or 201 [816/7])—65. A celebrated Sufi of the Baghdad school. He taught Sarī al-Saqaṭī, who was the teacher of al-Junayd. His parents are believed to have been Christians or Sabians. He was famous for his emphasis on the virtues of generosity and devotedness. (*SEI*, 327 [R.A. Nicholson]; Hujwīrī, 113–5; Qushayrī, I. 60–3; Sulamī, 74–9.)

MĀLIK IBN DĪNĀR, Abū Yaḥyā al-Sāmī al-Nājī (d. 131 [748/9])—42–3. A *tābʿī* and a famous ascetic and scholar in Basra. (*GAS*, I. 634.)

MAYMŪNA bint al-Ḥārith al-Hilālīya—57. The last wife that the Prophet married. She survived him by 27 years. She was also the sister-in-law of al-ʿAbbās. (Zabīdī, v. 63; *SEI*, 315 [F. Buhl].)

MUʿĀDH IBN JABAL, Abū ʿAbd al-Raḥmān ibn ʿAmr ibn Aws al-Khazrajī (d. 17 [638/9] or 18 [639/40])—9, 37. A *ṣaḥābī* who was among the first converts to Islam. In spite of his young age, he was respected for his religious knowledge. (Dhahabī, *Tadhkira*, I. 19–22; Shīrāzī, *Ṭabaqāt*, 14–5.)

MUḤAMMAD IBN ḤASSĀN ibn Fīrūz al-Baghdādī (d. 257 [870/1])—65. A traditionist. (Zabīdī, v. 70.)

MUJĀHID, Abu'l-Ḥajjāj ibn Jabr al-Makkī (d. 104 [722/3])—21, 33. A *tābiʿī* and disciple of Ibn ʿAbbās. He was a scholar of the highest authority in *fiqh* and Qur'ānic exegesis, representing the rationalistic trend in these branches. (*GAS*, I. 29.)

MUṢʿAB IBN SAʿD, Abū Zarūʿa ibn Abī Waqqāṣ al-Zuhrī (d. 102 [720/1] or 103 [721/2])—20. A *tābiʿī*. (Nawawī, *Tahdhīb*, 555–6; Zabīdī, v. 18.)

AL-NUʿMĀN IBN BASHĪR, Abū ʿAbd Allāh ibn Saʿd al-Khazrajī (d. 74 [693/4])—17, 31. He served the Umayyad Caliph Yazīd as governor of Kufa and Ḥimṣ, but later joined the revolt of ʿAbd Allāh ibn al-Zubayr and was killed. (Zabīdī, v. 14; *EI*, III. 952–3 [K. V. Zettersteen].)

QABĪṢA IBN AL-MUKHĀRIQ, Abū Bishr ibn ᶜAbd Allāh ibn Shaddād al-Hilālī—62. A *ṣaḥābī*. He narrated some other traditions related to natural phenomena like the solar eclipse. No death date is given. (*Iṣāba*, iii. 215; Nawawī, *Tahdhīb*, 509; Ibn Durayd, *Ishtiqāq*, 178.)

QATĀDA, Abū 'l-Khaṭṭāb ibn Diᶜāma ibn Qatāda al-Sadūsī (d. 118 [736/7])—55. A *tābiᶜī*, exegete and *faqīh*. He was also a great expert in Arab poetry. (*GAS*, i. 31–2; Dhahabī, *Tadhkira*, i. 122–4.)

RĀBIᶜA AL-ᶜADAWĪYA (d. 185 [801/2])—55. A famous Ṣūfīya of Basra especially noted for her teaching on mystic love (*maḥabba*) and intimacy (*uns*) with God; her life was one of extreme asceticism and otherworldiness. (*SEI*, 462–63 [M. Smith]; idem, *Rābiᶜa the Mystic*.)

Al-RABĪᶜ IBN KHUTHAYM, Abū Yazīd ibn ᶜĀ'idh ibn ᶜAbd Allāh al-Thawrī al-Kūfī (d. *c* 63 [682/3])—55. A *tābiᶜī* and disciple of Ibn Masᶜūd noted for his piety. There is some confusion about his name. All the texts have Ibn Khaytham. (See also Tāshköprüzāde, ii. 21.) Zabīdī himself, however, mentions his name as Ibn Khuthaym in another place (Zabīdī, iii. 167) and explains that this is a diminutive form. Other biographers have this correct form. (*Tahdhīb al-Tahdhīb*, iii. 242–3; Ibn Durayd, *Ishtiqāq*, 112–13.)

RIFĀᶜA AL-ZARQĪ, Abū Muᶜādh ibn Rāfiᶜ ibn Mālik (d. 41 [661/2])—16. A *ṣaḥābī* and narrator of Tradition. (Nawawī, *Tahdhīb*, 246–7.)

SAᶜDŪN AL-MAJNŪN—44. It is said that he became a lunatic during half of the year and returned to normal during the other half. (Shaᶜrānī, i. 68.)

SAᶜĪD IBN JUBAYR, Abū ᶜAbd Allāh (or Abū Muḥammad) ibn Hishām al-Asadī (d. 95 [713/4])—42. A *tābiᶜī* noted for his piety and learning in exegesis, Tradition and *fiqh*. He was killed by al-Ḥajjāj ibn Yūsuf. (Ibn Khallikān, I. 564–7; Nawawī, *Tahdhīb*, 278–79.)

SALAMA IBN AL-AKWAᶜ, ᶜAmr (d. 64 [683/4] or 74 [693/4])—41. A *ṣaḥābī*. His son said of him, 'My father never told a lie'. (*Iṣāba*, II. 65; Nawawī, *Tahdhīb*, 295–96.)

SALMĀN Al-FĀRISĪ (d. *c* 35 [655/6])—34. One of the most popular figures of Muslim legends. (*SEI*, 500–1 [G. Levi della Vida].)

SAMURA IBN JUNDUB al-Fazārī (d. 51–60 [671/2–679/80])—18. A *ṣaḥābī* and one of the eminent narrators of Tradition. (Zabīdī, V. 15; *GAS*, I. 84–5.)

AL-SHĀFIᶜĪ, Abū ᶜAbd Allāh Muḥammad ibn Idrīs ibn al-ᶜAbbās (d. 204 [820])—50. The founder of the Shāfiᶜite *madhhab*. (*GAS*, I. 484–90; *SEI*, 512–5 [W. Heffening].)

SUFYĀN AL-THAWRĪ, Abū ᶜAbd Allāh ibn Saᶜīd (or Saᶜd) ibn Masrūq al-Kūfī (d. 161 777/8])—42. A celebrated traditionist, theologian, and ascetic. He founded an independent *madhhab*, but it did not last long. He was one of those pious men who showed their dislike of the new Umayyad regime by refusing offices in government service. (*EI*, IV. 500–2 [M. Plessner]; *GAS*, I. 518–19.)

SUFYĀN IBN ᶜUYAYNA, Abū Muḥammad ibn Maymūn al-Hilālī (d. 196 [811/2] or 198 [813/4])—10, 39. A great traditionist and exegete. (*GAS*, I. 96; Zabīdī, V. 9.)

THĀBIT AL-BUNĀNĪ, Abū Muḥammad ibn Aslam al-Baṣrī (d. 123 [740/1] or 127 [744/5])—5. One of the most eminent Followers (*tābiᶜī*) and a pious narrator of Tradition, who is said to have recited the whole Qur'ān every day. (*Tahdhīb al-Tahdhīb*, II. 2–4.)

ᶜUBĀDA IBN AL-ṢĀMIT, Abu'l-Walīd ibn Qays al-Khazrajī (d. 34 [654/5] or 45 [665/6])—15. A *ṣaḥābī* and a famous narrator of Tradition. He was the first judge of Syria, and one of those who collected the revelations during the Prophet's lifetime. (Ibn Qutayba, *Ma^c^ārif*, 131; *Iṣāba*, II. 260–1.)

^c^UMAR ibn al-Khaṭṭāb (d. 23 [644])—27, 35, 46, 48. The second Caliph. One of the greatest figures of the early days of Islam and the founder of the Arab Empire. (*SEI*, 600–1 [G. Levi della Vida].)

^c^UTBA AL-GHULĀM, Abū ^c^Abd Allāh ibn Abān ibn Sam^c^a (d. before 153 [770/1])—65. He was nicknamed al-Ghulām as he was a servant (*ghulām*), not because he was young. A celebrated saint of Baṣra. His state of sorrow (*ḥuzn*) is compared to that of al-Hasan al-Baṣrī. (*Tahdhīb al-Tahdhīb*, I. 95, Abū Nu^c^aym, VI. 226–38; Sha^c^rānī, I. 47; Hujwīrī, 180.)

YAḤYĀ AL-GHASSĀNĪ, Abū Zakarīyā ibn Hāshim ibn Kathīr ibn Qays—44. A traditionist. According to al-Khaṭīb al-Baghdādī (*Tārīkh Baghdād*, XIV. 164–5) and Ibn Ḥajar (*Lisān al-mīzān*, VI. 279–80), he was not very trustworthy because 'he was writing down Traditions and stealing them'. He learned Tradition from al-A^c^mash (d. *c* 148) and others. No death date is given. (See also Ibn al-Jazarī, *Ghāya*, II. 379–80.)

YŪNUS IBN ^c^UBAYD, Abū ^c^Abd Allāh (or Abū ^c^Ubayd) ibn Dīnār al-^c^Abdi al-Baṣrī (d. 139 [756/7])—67. A traditionist who was a disciple of al-Ḥasan al-Baṣrī. He was older than Sulaymān al-Taymī. (Zabīdī, V. 72; *GAS*, I. 88.)

YUSAYRA—20. A *ṣaḥābīya*. Her *kunya* is given as Umm Yāsir, and some called her Yusayra bint Yāsir. (Zabīdī, V. 17.)

APPENDIX II

SOME IMPORTANT INVOCATIONS

1. *Subḥān Allāh*: the proclamation that God is completely free from every impurity and imperfection. Syntactically, *subḥān* is the verbal noun in the form of *fuᶜlān* (e.g. *ghufrān*) and put in the accusative form (*manṣūb*) as the object of a verb which is suppressed. Hence literally it means: '[I proclaim] the glory of God!' According to Jurjānī,[A] this *tasbīḥ* is more general than *taqdīs*, or the uttering of God's holiness,[B] in its proclamation of God's transcendence. It is used in the Qur'ān to express the impression made by God's overwhelming greatness and His wondrous deeds, or to deny anything contradictory to His absolute perfection and superiority (Bayḍāwī, *Tafsīr*, 23; E.W. Lane, *Lexicon*, IV. 1289–90; F. Buhl, 'Subḥān Allāh', *EI*, IV. 492–3; C.E. Padwick, *Muslim Devotions*, 65–74).

2. *al-ḥamdu li'Llāh*: the proclamation that praise belongs to God for all His favours. Lexicographically, *ḥamd*, meaning 'praise', 'eulogy', is used for a certain excellent voluntary (*ikhtiyārī*) deed of man—either a favour or an excellent performance and the like—as distinguished from *madḥ*, which has no such connotation. When used in relation to the former, it comes to have the same meaning as *shukr* (thanks). All are from God, and He is to be praised and thanked for all these as His favours to man, pleasant or grievous—pleasant because of pleasantness, and grievous because of the hidden Wisdom

[A] *Taᶜrīfāt*, 29.

[B] Unlike *tasbīḥ* this does not have a fixed formula.

(*ḥikma*) of God. This is what Ghazālī means by this phrase.[A] *Tasbīḥ* is the praise of God, the Transcendent, and *taḥmīd* is the praise of God, the Donor of gifts and favours. For more details, see Tahānawī, II. 88–90; Bayḍāwī, 3; Jurjānī, 41–2; Lane, *Lexicon*, II. 638–39; D.B.Macdonald, art. 'Ḥamdala', in *EI²*, III. 122–3; C.E. Padwick, *Muslim Devotions*, 75–82; E.W. Lane, 'Aus einem Briefe', *ZDMG*, 20 (1865), 187–88.

3. *Allāhu akbar*: the proclamation that God is incomparably greater than any other being. The Qur'ān does not have this formula as it stands, although it is implied in some places, e.g. *kabbirhu takbīr[an]* (XVII:111). Syntactically there are several explanations given to this *takbīr*-formula. Some take *akbar* in the sense of *kabīr*, although this explanation is weak. It is mostly understood that this phrase is elliptical, since *akbar* lacks the article. Some take this as meaning *akbar kabīr* (greater than [any] great [being]); some *akbar min kull shay'* (greater than any [other] thing); some *akbar min an yuʿraf kunh kibriyā'ih wa-ʿaẓamatih* (too great for the measure of His grandeur and majesty to be known) (Lane, *Lexicon*, VII. 2587; Ibn Manẓūr, *Lisān al-ʿarab*, V. 127). On the other hand, some Western scholars see a parallel to this ejaculation in the similar Jewish worship (*Tᵉphillā*).[B] Others see in the reiterated *takbīr* of the *adhān* 'a shout of defiance, a word of power, against the dethroned heathen gods'[C] and resentful demonic forces, ousted by the new worship of God.

[A] *Iḥyā'*, I. 168 (*K. al-Ṣalāt*, bāb 3, Bayān tafṣīl . . .); IV, 79–82 (*K. al-Ṣabr wa'l-shukr*, shaṭr 2, Bayān ḥadd al-shukr).

[B] E.M. Mittwoch, 'Entstehungsgeschichte', 16–17.

[C] C.E. Padwick, *Muslim Devotions*, 30. See also A.J. Wensinck, art. 'Takbīr' in *EI*, IV. 627; *Iḥyā'*, I. 152–5 (*K. al-Ṣalāt*, bāb 2, al-Qirā'a—al-Sujūd).

INDEX TO QUR'ĀNIC QUOTATIONS

BIBLIOGRAPHY

(The following are the titles referred to in this book)

[c]Abd al-Bāqī, Muḥammad Fu'ād. *al-Mu[c]jam al-Mufahras li-alfāẓ al-Qur'ān al-Karīm*. [Cairo,] 1378 AH.

[c]Abd al-Razzāq. *Kitāb iṣṭilāḥāt al-ṣūfīya*. Ed. Aloys Sprenger. Calcutta, 1845.

Abū Dāūd. *al-Sunan*. Cairo, 1369–70/1950–1.

Arberry, Arthur John. *The Koran Interpreted*. New York, [1955?].

——*The Doctrine of the Sufis*. [Tr. of Kalābādhī's *Ta[c]arruf*.] Cambridge, 1953.

——*Muslim Saints and Mystics. Episodes from the Tadhkirat al-Auliya' ("Memorial of the Saints") by Farid al-Din Attar*. Chicago, 1966.

Bayḍāwī, [c]Abd Allāh b. [c]Umar, al-. *Tafsīr al-Qur'ān al-Karīm*. [= *Anwār al-tanzīl wa-asrār al-ta'wīl*.] Cairo, n.d.

Bell, Richard. *The Qur'ān Translated with a Critical Re-arrangement of the Surahs*. Edinburgh, 1937.

Bousquet, George Henri (ed. and tr.). *Études islamologiques d'Ignaz Goldziher*. See under Goldziher.

Bouyges, Maurice. *Essai de chronologie des oeuvres de al-Ghazālī (Algazel)*. Edited and revised by Michael Allard. Beirut, 1959.

Brockelmann, Carl. *Geschichte der arabischen Litteratur*. 2nd ed. Leiden, 1943–49; *Supplement*, 1937–42.

Bukhārī, Muḥammad b. Ismā[c]īl, al-. *al-Jāmi[c] al-Ṣaḥīḥ*. Edited by M. Ludolf Krehl and Theodor W. Juynboll. Leiden, 1862–1908.

Calverley, Edwin Elliot. *Worship in Islam: Being a Translation, with Commentary and Introduction of al-Ghazzálí's Book of the Iḥyá' on the Worship*. 2nd [revised] ed. London, 1957.

Daylamī, Abū Shujāʿ Shīrawayh, al-. *al-Firdaws bi-ma'thūr al-khiṭāb*. Ed. al-Saʿīd Zaghlūl. Beirut, 1406/1986.

Dhahabī, Muḥammad b. Aḥmad, al-. *Tadhkirat al-ḥuffāẓ*. Hyderabad, 1333–34 AH.

——*Tajrīd asmā' al-ṣaḥāba*. Hyderabad, 1315 AH.

——*Mīzān al-iʿtidāl fī naqd al-rijāl*. Cairo, 1963.

Encyclopedia of Islam, The. Ed. by M. Houtsma *et al*. Leiden, 1927. New edition, ed. by J.H. Kramers, H.A.R. Gibb *et al*. Leiden, 1954- .

Encyclopaedia of Religion and Ethics, The. Edited by James Hastings. New York, 1908–27.

Fīrūzābādī, Abū Ṭāhir, al-. *Tanwīr al-miqbās min tafsīr Ibn ʿAbbās*. Cairo, 1370/1951.

Gardet, Louis. 'Un problème de mystique comparée. La mention du nom divin (*dhikr*) dans la mystique musulmane.' *RT*, 52 (1952), 642–79; 53 (1953), 197–216.

Ghazālī, Abū Ḥāmid Muḥammad b. Muḥammad, al-. *Iḥyā' ʿulūm al-dīn*. Cairo: ʿĪsā al-Bābī al-Ḥalabī, n.d; Cairo: Lajna Nashr al-Thaqāfat al-Islāmīya, 1356–57 AH.

——*K. al-imlā' fī ishkālāt al-Iḥyā'*. In margin of *Iḥyā'* (Cairo: ʿĪsā al-Ḥalabī, n.d.), I. 55–203.

——*K. al-arbaʿīn fī uṣūl al-dīn*. Cairo, 1344/1925.

——*al-Munqidh min al-ḍalāl wa'l-mūṣil ilā dhi al-ʿizza wa'l-jalāl*. Arabic text and French translation by Farid Jabre, Beirut, 1959.

——*K. al-Wajīz fī fiqh madhhab al-Imām al-Shāfiʿī*. Cairo, 1317 AH.

——*Bidāyat al-hidāya*. Cairo, n.d.

——*K. al-Ḥikma fī makhlūqāt Allāh*. In *al-Rasā'il al-farā'id*. (Cairo, n.d.), 15–96.

——*al-Adab fī al-dīn*. In *Majmūʿat al-rasā'il* (Cairo, 1328 AH), 64–94.

——*K. Kīmiyā' al-saʿāda*. Tehran, 1960.

Gibb, Hamilton A.R. *Mohammedanism: An Historical Survey*. New York, 1962.

Goldziher, Ignaz. *Le dogme et la loi de l'Islam: histoire du développement dogmatique et juridique de la religion musulmane*. Translated by Félix Arin. New ed. Paris, 1958.

——*Gesammelte Schriften*. Edited by Joseph DeSomogyi. Hildesheim, 1967.

——*Abhandlungen zur arabischen Philologie*. [2 parts.] Leiden, 1896–99.

——*Études islamologiques d'Ignaz Goldziher*. Edited and translated by G.H. Bousquet. Leiden, 1962.

——'Einige arabische Ausrufe und Formeln.' *WZKM*, 16 (1902) 131–46.

——'Arabische Synonymik der Askese.' *Der Islam*, 8 (1918), 210–13.

——'Hyperbolische Typen im Arabischen.' in *Gesammelte Schriften*, III (1969), 33–49.

——'Über die Vorgeschichte der Hiǧā'-Poesie.' *Abhandlungen zur arabischen Philologie*. [Part I] 1–121.

——'Über die Eulogien der Muhammedaner.' *ZDMG*, 50 (1896), 97–128.

——'Zauberelemente im islamischen Gebet.' *Orientalische Studien Theodor Nöldeke zum Siebzigsten Geburtstag (2 März 1906) Gewidmet von Freunden und Schülern*. Ed. Carl Bezold. Giessen, 1906, I. 303–29.

——'Über eine rituelle Formel der Muhammedaner.' *ZDMG*, 48 (1894), 95–100.

Goldziher, Ignaz. 'Bismillāh.' *ERE*, II. 666–8.

Haas, William S. 'The Zikr of the Rahmanija-Order in Algeria: A Psycho-Physiological Analysis.' *MW*, 33 (1943), 16–28.

Ḥājjī K͟halīfa. *Kas͟hf al-ẓunūn ᶜan asāmī al-kutub wa'l-funūn*. Ed. Gustav Flügel. London, 1835–58.

Ḥākim al-Nīsābūrī, al-. *al-Mustadrak ᶜalā al-Ṣaḥīḥayn*. Hyderabad, 1334–42 AH.

Haythamī, ᶜAlī b. Abī Bakr, al-. *Majmaᶜ al-zawāʾid wa-manbaᶜ al-fawāʾid*. Cairo, 1352 AH.

Heiler, Friedrich. *Das Gebet: eine religionsgeschichtliche und religionspsychologische Untersuchung*. Munich, 1923.

Hughes, Thomas Patrick. *Dictionary of Islam*. London, 1885.

Ibn al-Athīr. *Tajrīd asmāʾ al-ṣaḥāba*. Hyderabad, 1315 AH.

——*al-Lubāb fī tahdhīb al-ansāb*. Cairo, 1357–69 AH.

Ibn Durayd, Muḥammad b. al-Ḥasan. *K. al-ishtiqāq*. Ed. F. Wüstenfeld. Göttingen, 1854.

Ibn Ḥajar al-ᶜAsqalānī. *al-Iṣāba fī tamyīz al-ṣaḥāba*. Cairo, 1358/1939.

——*Lisān al-mīzān*. Hyderabad, 1329–31 AH.

——*Tahdhīb al-tahdhīb*. Hyderabad, 1325–7 AH.

Ibn Ḥanbal, Aḥmad. *al-Musnad*. Cairo, 1373–6/1954–6.

Ibn al-Jazarī, Shams al-Dīn Muḥammad. *Ghāyat al-nihāya fī ṭabaqāt al-qurrāʾ*. Ed. G. Bergsträsser and O. Pretzl. Cairo, 1351–2/1932–3.

Ibn Khallikān, Aḥmad. *Wafayāt al-aᶜyān wa-anbāʾ al-zamān*. Trans. William MacGuckin de Slane. Paris, 1842–71.

Ibn Māja al-Qazwīnī. *al-Sunan*. Ed. Muḥammad Fuʾād ᶜAbd al-Bāqī. Cairo, 1372–3/1952–4.

Ibn Manẓūr, Muḥammad. *Lisān al-ᶜArab*. Beirut, 1374–76/1955–56.

Ibn Qutayba, ᶜAbd Allāh b. Muslim. *al-Maᶜārif*. Ed. F. Wüstenfeld. Göttingen, 1850.

Ibn Saᶜd, Muḥammad. *al-Ṭabaqāt al-kabīr*. Ed. E. Sachau *et al.* Leiden, 1322–47/1905–28.

Ibn al-Sunnī, Abū Bakr. *ᶜAmal al-yawm wa'l-layla*. Ed. ᶜAbdallāh Ḥajjāj. Cairo, 1982.

Ibn Taghribirdī, Abu'l-Maḥāsin. *Al-Nujūm al-zāhira fī mulūk Miṣr wa'l-Qāhira*. Cairo, 1348–58/1929–39.

Iṣfahānī, Abū Nuᶜaym, al-. *Ḥilyat al-awliyāʾ wa-ṭabaqāt al-asfiyāʾ*. Cairo, 1351–7/1932–8. Reprinted Beirut, 1387/1969.

Jabre, Farid. *La notion de certitude selon Ghazali dans ses origines psychologiques et historiques*. Paris, 1958.

——'La biographie et l'oeuvre de Ghazālī réconsidérées à la lumière des Ṭabaqāt de Sobkī.' *MIDEO* 1 (1954), 73–102.

Jurjānī, ᶜAlī b. Muḥammad, al-. *al-Taᶜrīfāt*. Cairo, 1306 AH.

Kaḥḥāla, ᶜUmar Riḍā. *Muᶜjam al-mu'allifīn: tarājim muṣannifī al-kutub al-ᶜarabīya*. Damascus, 1376–80/1957–61.

Kalābādhī, Muḥammad b. Isḥāq, al-. *al-Taᶜarruf li-madhhab ahl al-taṣawwuf*. Ed. ᶜAbd al-Ḥalīm Maḥmūd and Ṭāhā ᶜAbd al-Bāqī Surūr, 1380/1960.

Khadduri, Majid. *Islamic Jurisprudence: Shāfi'ī's* Risāla. Baltimore (USA), 1961.

Khaṭīb al-Baghdādī, al-. *Tārīkh Baghdād*. Cairo, 1349 AH.

Lane, Edward William. *An Arabic-English Lexicon*. London, 1863–93.

——*The Manners and Customs of the Modern Egyptians*. London, repr. 1966.

——'Aus einem Briefe von Edw. Wm. Lane an Prof. Fleischer.' *ZDMG* 20 (1865), 187–88.

Laoust, Henri. *La politique de Ġazālī*. Paris, 1970.

Macdonald, Duncan Black. 'The Life of al-Ghazzālī with Especial Reference to His Religious Experiences and Opinions.' *JAOS*, 20 (1899), 71–132.

——*The Religious Attitude and Life in Islam*. Chicago, 1909.

Makkī, Abū Ṭālib, al-. *Qūt al-qulūb fī muᶜāmala al-Maḥbūb wa-waṣf ṭarīq al-murīd ilā maqām al-tawḥīd*. Cairo, 1381/1961.

Massignon, Louis. *Essai sur les origines du lexique technique de la mystique musulmane*. [Revised ed.] Paris, 1954.

McKane, William. *Al-Ghazālī's Book of Fear and Hope*. [Translation of the *K. al-Khawf wa'l-rajā'* of the *Iḥyā'*.] Leiden, 1965.

Mittwoch, Eugen. 'Zur Entstehungsgeschichte des islamischen Gebets.' *Abhandlungen der königlich-preussischen Akademie der Wissenschaften*, Philosophisch-Historische Classe, 1913, 1–42.

Muslim b. al-Ḥajjāj. *al-Jāmiᶜ al-Ṣaḥīḥ*. Cairo, 1334 AH. al-Nasā'ī, Aḥmad. *al-Sunan*. Cairo, 1383–4/1964–5.

Nawawī, Muḥyi'l-Dīn Yaḥyā, al-. *Tahdhīb al-asmā' wa'l-lughāt*. Ed. F. Wüstenfeld. Göttingen, 1842–7.

Nicholson, R.A. *The Kashf al-maḥjúb: the oldest Persian treatise on Sufiism*. [Tr. with introduction of the *Kashf al-Maḥjūb* of al-Jullābī al-Hujwīrī.] (E.J.W. Gibb Memorial Series, Vol. XVII.) [repr.] London, 1936.

Padwick, Constance E. *Muslim Devotions: A Study of Prayer-Manuals in Common Use*. London, 1961.

Pickthall, Mohammed Marmaduke. *The Meaning of the Glorious Koran*. [10th ed.] New York, 1963.

Qushayrī, Abu'l-Qāsim, al-. *al-Risāla al-Qushayrīya*. Ed. ᶜAbd al-Ḥalīm Maḥmūd and Maḥmūd b. al-Sharīf. Cairo, 1385/1966.

Rodwell, John Medows. *The Koran Translated from the Arabic*. London, 1909.

Schaya, L. 'The Eliatic Function'. *SCR* 1979, 15–38.

Schimmel, Annemarie. 'Some Aspects of Mystical Prayer in Islam.' *Die Welt des Islams*, N.S. II (1952), 112–25.

Sezgin, Fuat. *Geschichte des arabischen Schrifttums*. Leiden, 1967–.

Shorter Encyclopaedia of Islam. Ed. H.A.R. Gibb and J.H. Kramers. Leiden, 1953.

Shaᶜrānī, ᶜAbd al-Wahhāb, al-. *al-Ṭabaqāt al-Kubrā*. Cairo, 1373/1954.

Shīrāzī, Abū Isḥāq, al-. *al-Tanbīh fī al-fiqh ᶜalā madhhab al-Imām al-Shāfiᶜī*. Cairo, 1370/1951.

——*Ṭabaqāt al-Fuqahā'*. Published with Ibn Hidāya, *Ṭabaqāt al-Shāfiᶜīya*. Baghdad, 1338 AH.

Smith, Margaret. *Rābiᶜa the Mystic and Her Fellow Saints in Islam*. Cambridge, 1928.

——*An Early Mystic of Baghdad: A study of the Life and Teaching of Ḥārith B. Asad al-Muḥāsibī A.D. 781–A.D.857*. London, 1935.

Sulamī, Abū ^{c}Abd al-Raḥmān, al. *Ṭabaqāt al-ṣūfīya*. Ed. J. Pedersen. Leiden, 1960.

Suyūṭī, Jalāl al-Dīn, al-, and Maḥallī, Jalāl al-Dīn, al-, *Tafsīr al-Qur'ān al-Karīm* [= *Tafsīr al-Jalālayn*]. Cairo, 1966.

Ṭabarānī, Sulayman b. Aḥmad, al-. *al-Mu^{c}jam al-ṣaghīr*. Ed. ^{c}Abd al-Raḥmān Muḥammad ^{c}Uthmān. [2nd ed.] Medina, 1388/1968.

——*al-Mu^{c}jam al-Kabīr*. Baghdad,

Ṭabarī, Ibn Jarīr, al-. *Jāmi^{c} al-bayān fī ta'wīl āī al-Qur'ān*. Cairo, [1321?].

Tahānawī, al-. *Kashshāf iṣṭilāḥāt al-funūn*. Ed. Aloys Sprenger and W. Nassau Lees. [Repr.] Beirut, 1966.

Tāshköprüzāde. *Miftāḥ al-sa^{c}āda wa-miṣbāḥ al-siyāda fī mawḍū^{c}āt al-^{c}ulūm*. Ed. Kāmil Kāmil Bakīr and ^{c}Abd al-Wahhāb Abu'l-Nūr. Cairo, n.d.

Tibawi, Abdul Latif. 'Al-Ghazali's Tract of Dogmatic Theology, Edited, Translated, Annotated, and Introduced.' *IQ* IX (1965), 65–122.

Tirmidhī, al-. *al-Sunan*. Medina, 1384–7/1964–7.

Wāqidī, Muḥammad b. ^{c}Umar, al-. *al-Maghāzī*. Ed. Marsden Jones. Cairo, 1966.

Watt, W. Montgomery. *Muslim Intellectual: A study of al-Ghazali*. Edinburgh, 1962.

——*The Faith and Practice of al-Ghazali*. [Includes the *Deliverance from Error and Attachment to the Lord of Might and Majesty*, and the *Beginning of Guidance*, which are translations of the *Munqidh* and the *Bidāya* of al-Ghazālī.] London, 1953.

Wellhausen, Julius. *Reste arabischen Heidentums*. [Rev. ed.] Berlin, 1927.

Wensinck, Arent Jan. *The Muslim Creed: Its Genesis and Historical Development*. Cambridge, 1932.

——*La Pensée de Ghazzālī*. Paris, 1940.

——'On the Relation between Ghazālī's Cosmology and His Mysticism.' *Mededeelingen der Koninklijke Akademie van*

Wetenschappen, Afdeeling Letterkunde, Ser. A, 75 (1933), 183–209.

Westermarck, Edward. *Ritual and Belief in Morocco.* [Repr.] New York, 1968.

Winter, T.J. *Al-Ghazālī. The Remembrance of Death and the Afterlife.* [Translation of the *K. Dhikr al-mawt* from the *Iḥyā'*.] Cambridge, 1989.

Yāfiʿī, al-. *Mir'āt al-janān wa-ʿibrat al-yaqẓān.* Hyderabad, 1337–8.

Zabīdī, al-Sayyid al-Murtaḍā al-. *Itḥāf al-sādat al-muttaqīn bi-sharḥ asrār Iḥyā' ʿulūm al-dīn.* Cairo, 1311 AH.

Zamakhsharī, Jār Allāh, al-. *al-Kashshāf ʿan ḥaqā'iq al-tanzīl wa-ʿuyūn al-aqāwīl fī wujūh al-ta'wīl.* Cairo, 1385/1966.

Zwemer, Samuel M. *Studies in Popular Islam.* London, 1939.

GENERAL INDEX

Islamic Texts Society
Al-Ghazālī Series
General Editor: T J Winter

1 **The Remembrance of Death and the Afterlife** (*Kitāb Dhikr al-mawt wa-mā baʿdahu.*) Translated with an Introduction and Notes by T J Winter, 1989.